What Makes America TICK?

A Multiskill Approach to English through U.S. Culture and History

SECOND EDITION

WENDY ASHBY

Ann Arbor
The University of Michigan Press

ISBN 978-0-472-03494-9

Published in the United States of America by
The University of Michigan Press

2015   2014   2013   2012   4   3   2   1

This book is dedicated to all the people who make America what it is.

Acknowledgments

Grateful acknowledgments are made to the following authors, collections, publishers, and photographers for granting permission to use images or to reprint previously published materials.

DoD Visual Information Record Center for the following photos: the White House; the Vietnam Veterans Memorial; the space shuttle; the Berlin Wall; President Wilson addresses Congress; Duke Ellington; "We Can Do It!"; Confederate lines near Chattanooga Railroad; Abraham Lincoln; President Johnson greets American troops; tank moves through Saigon.

Library of Congress, Prints and Photographs Division, for the following photos: immigrant family looking at Statue of Liberty from Ellis Island; workers in Canton Glass Works, Marion, Indiana; a suffragist works to win the vote; representative with flappers doing the Charleston; young man in dustbowl; a migrant mother; woman and two children; teens learn rock 'n' roll; teenage girls and Elvis movie poster; Martin Luther King, Jr.; poster for Woodstock Festival; First Lady Jacqueline Kennedy; 1960s civil rights protest.

Penguin Putnam, Inc., for excerpts from Upton Sinclair's *The Jungle.* Copyright © 1905, 1906 by Upton Sinclair. Used by permission of Viking Penguin, a division of Penguin Putnam Inc.

Smithsonian American Art Museum, Transfer from the U.S. Department of Labor, for *Industry* by Arthur Durston. Copyright © 1934 NMAA.

U.S. National Archives and Records Administration for *Mother and Boy at Table,* photo by Arnold Eagle and David Robbins. Copyright © 1938 National Archives and Records Administration.

U.S. Navy for photo of the New York City firemen by Journalist 1st Class Preston Keres.

Don Ward for photos of Franklin D. Roosevelt statue.

Contents

8 **The U.S. Enters the 21st Century: Diversity versus Unity**   **147**
     in a Rapidly Shifting World

To the Instructor

What Makes America Tick? is a comprehensive package of instructional materials for intermediate and high-intermediate students of English. It is a systematic bridge into simple advanced skills that focuses on integrated reading, writing, speaking, and listening within an authentic context based on culture, vocabulary, and sociolinguistic appropriateness. Critical relationships among all elements of language are explored. The controlling philosophy is that lower-proficiency language students should be offered the opportunity to study language as it applies to higher-level thinking activities. Such activities should be based on cultural artifacts such as art, music, literature, and history of the target culture. These higher-level topics have traditionally been reserved for those students who already possess advanced-level vocabulary and structures.

The objectives of this textbook are to:

- improve reading skills by engaging learners in readings that give an overview of important events in 20th century U.S. history
- increase learner proficiency in high-frequency vocabulary words and improve skills in defining and using their derivatives
- improve formal and informal writing skills via personal responses to events portrayed in the text and in optional journal keeping
- improve formal presentation, informal discussion, and speaking skills via both in-class discussions and more structured peer interview situations
- enhance listening skills via peer and instructor interaction
- introduce students to academic concepts such as footnotes and summarizing by incorporating them throughout the text
- expose learners to and provide practice opportunities for sociolinguistically appropriate usages of U.S. American English
- provide interaction with authentic cultural artifacts from the 20th century, including literature, poetry, artwork, sculpture, photography, and speeches, and to make explicit their contextual importance

- create opportunities for learning and putting into practice a working knowledge of significant and relevant historical events, as well as understanding their relationships to current U.S. American institutions, politics, attitudes, and values.

What Makes America Tick? consists of eight units. Each unit contains a level-appropriate reading; authentic photos; vocabulary lists and activities; various cloze and open-response activities for reading, speaking, listening, and writing; a Language Focus activity; and a Link to Today section that examines the current effects of history on people's lives. Classroom activities engage students in meaningful, cross-cultural, information-gap comparisons of politics, attitudes, and values with the aim of eliciting their observations of and reactions to various policies, movements, and events in U.S. American history. Students have the opportunity to both learn about external culture as well as explore their experiences within and relationships to it.

It was not possible to include every significant historical event in the 20th century, so the focus is on those events that have left cultural imprints throughout the century and ones with the most far-reaching social implications. Every effort was made to ensure that this text is as culturally rich and authentic as possible, but copyright constraints made it difficult to include everything we would have liked to include. As a result, instructors are prompted to guide students to Internet sites to view some authentic pieces of art, such as the Andy Warhol Museum or the King Center, or for other information to support the readings and discussions. Departing from and/or supplementing material according to instructor and student interest is encouraged.

To the Student

What Makes America Tick? was designed especially for intermediate and high-intermediate students of English. It offers students who are developing their language skills a fun, interesting, and intellectual way to study English and U.S. American culture and history. The title of the book is an English idiom. It refers to old-fashioned watches that made a ticking sound when you wound them up. The moving parts inside the watch *made it tick.* When you want to know what *makes someone tick,* it means that you are puzzled or curious about this person and want to understand the inner workings of how this person thinks, feels, and operates. It is helpful for students studying in the United States to understand not only how the average U.S. American citizen thinks, feels, and operates, but also why. Demonstrating cultural understanding is one of the skills that can advance students to a higher-level course and greater fluency.

The objectives of the book are for you to:

- improve reading skills through interesting texts
- learn new, high-frequency vocabulary words
- gain better formal and informal writing skills
- obtain more advanced speaking and presentation skills
- participate effectively in group discussions
- learn and practice appropriate uses of U.S. American English
- examine authentic cultural artifacts such as: literature, poetry, artwork, sculpture, photography, and speeches, and to understand why they are important to U.S. citizens or to U.S. history
- develop a working knowledge of the history of the United States in the 20th century and the important events that shaped more current U.S. American politics, institutions, values, and attitudes.

What Makes America Tick? has eight units. Each unit contains activities for reading, speaking, listening, and writing. You will have opportunities to compare this information with that from your culture and community. Cultural artifacts such as pieces of art, literature, songs, and photos will help you to understand about past and present life in the United States. Each unit includes many examples of cultural artifacts that can be researched.

Presidential Suite

This section includes the names of U.S. presidents, their political party—Republican (R) or Democrat (D)—and the years they were in office. Search IPL POTUS (Presidents of the United States) for biographies and webpages for every United States president.

Music Box

This section lists some of the hit songs from the time period covered in the unit. One song that includes lyrics about many of the book's units is "We Didn't Start the Fire" by Billy Joel. This fast-paced hit from the 1980s takes the listener chronologically through multiple aspects of post–World War II history. Singers/songwriters are not included for all songs.

On TV and At the Movies

These sections include the names of television shows and movies that are set during the time period covered in the unit. One movie, *Forrest Gump,* looks at United States history through the eyes of one character as a boy in the 1950s, as a young man in the 1960s and '70s, and as a baby boomer in the 1980s and '90s.

Net Surfers

This section provides phrases you can search for online. For example, search the Internet for the phrase "History of the United States since 1865 syllabus." You should find listings and websites for undergraduate college courses and online history projects. Some are online course notes providing concise summaries and interesting photos.

1

The U.S. at the Beginning of the 20th Century

Immigration, Industry, and Social Reform

An immigrant family looks at the Statue of Liberty from Ellis Island. (Courtesy Library of Congress.)

In the beginning of the 20th century, the U.S. did not have a lot of big cities, but immigration continued. Despite small populations in rural towns, the U.S. was booming in industry. Social reform was inevitable with the growing population and the country's rise in industry.

Net Surfers

To learn more about the time period covered in this unit, search for these names, words, and phrases on the Internet.

child labor in New York City tenements, 1908

1930s Prohibition

immigration during the Progressive era

Pure Food and Drug Act

Ellis Island

Upton Sinclair

Food and Drug Administration

temperance movement

The Jungle (novel)

muckrakers

fast food

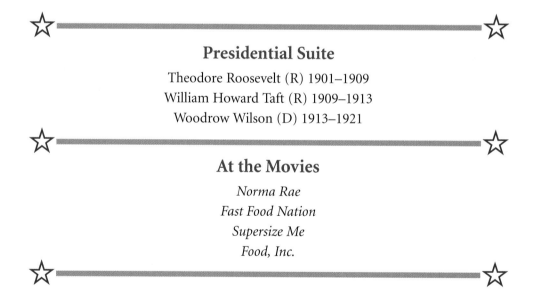

Presidential Suite

Theodore Roosevelt (R) 1901–1909

William Howard Taft (R) 1909–1913

Woodrow Wilson (D) 1913–1921

At the Movies

Norma Rae

Fast Food Nation

Supersize Me

Food, Inc.

Listening to different ideas, experiences, and opinions lays the foundations for opinion sharing and hypothesis formation that characterizes advanced English usage. Showing respect for others' ideas and experiences is also an important skill to gain and one that is highly valued in the United States. Sharing ideas about controversial issues provides a good way to practice showing respect for diversity through language.

Preparing to Read about the Rise of Large Industry and a Cry for Social Reform

Write some thoughts about these topics, and then discuss them with your classmates.

1. family's home country

   a. How big is your family's hometown? _____

   b. Describe the average apartment or house. _____

   _____

   c. What is the largest city you have lived in or visited? Did you like it? _____

   _____

   d. Describe the general living and working conditions in large cities. _____

   _____

2. social attitudes about the sale and use of alcohol

   a. What was the legal drinking age in other places that you have lived? _____

   b. What were the laws about drinking and driving in those places? Do you think they were too harsh or too lenient? _____

   _____

   c. What is the general public opinion on alcohol and alcoholism? _____

   _____

   d. Are there any groups who restrict or forbid the sale/use of alcoholic beverages?

   _____

   e. What types of consumables are restricted or forbidden where you live now?

   _____

3. social roles of men, women, and children

    a. Are men and women expected to act and behave differently in your family's home country? _____

    b. Is there anything that men or women are restricted from doing? _____

    _____

    c. What are the traditional roles related to having and raising children? Are they the same for your generation as for your parents' and grandparents'? _____

    _____

    d. Are children expected to contribute income to the family? If so, in what ways?

    _____

Learning New Vocabulary about the U.S. at the Beginning of the 20th Century

Although this is a long list of words to learn, these words will be helpful to understanding the reading. Review the vocabulary (in alphabetical order by part of speech) and definitions, and refer to this list as needed.

agriculture (n) farming

constitutional amendment (n) an addition to the U.S. Constitution; new ones can be added with a two-thirds vote by the Senate and the House of Representatives and approval by three-quarters of state governments. The first 10 constitutional amendments are called the *Bill of Rights.*

industrialization (n) the shift from a society based on agriculture to one based on factory work

monopoly (n) when one business or industry has no competition

muckrakers (n) name given to newspaper reporters who exposed bad things; refers to the person who cleans horse stalls

opposition (n) the state of being against something; action taken against a person or idea

suffrage (n) the right to vote

urbanization (n) shift from living on farms to living in cities

wage (n) pay; money received based on hourly work

to bribe (v) to give someone in an official position money or a gift to get what you need or to keep from being arrested for breaking the law

to exploit (v) to take advantage of

to expose (v) to shed light on something

to flock (v) to gather

to repeal (v) to take away or make powerless (law)

eligible (adj) qualified or meeting the requirements

moral (adj) good, right, or correct behavior in a society

underground (adj) hidden—not seen and usually illegal

vocal (adj) outspoken; making yourself heard

Talking about New Words and Concepts

Take some time to think and talk about new ideas associated with the vocabulary. Then use your understanding of the new vocabulary to discuss each set of the questions with a partner.

1. In the United States, the Constitution has an "elastic clause." This allows the laws to be changed or expanded to meet the needs of the people as society changes. For example, if an old law doesn't apply to society anymore, a new one can be made. These additions and changes to the Constitution are called *amendments*. *To amend* means "to change." A new amendment to the Constitution is suggested by the people and proposed as a bill. The bill is voted on by members of Congress in the Senate and the House of Representatives. If two-thirds of the congressional members vote for the bill, it can become a **constitutional amendment**. The amendment must also be passed by three-fourths of the state governments before it can become federal law. There is no limit on how many amendments the U.S. Constitution can have. The first ten amendments to the Constitution are called the *Bill of Rights*. The United States Constitution currently has 27 amendments.

   a. What are the benefits of such a system?

   b. What problems could it cause?

   c. What happens in your community if a law doesn't help people anymore?

   d. Is there a law in your home country that you think needs to be changed? What is it? How can the law be made better?

   e. List some words that are related to *amendment*.

2. When a person is very outspoken about a problem, he or she is said to be **vocal**. The word *vocal* is related to the word *voice*. Being vocal is generally a positive trait in U.S. society. People often ask others' opinions and encourage them to speak up for themselves and express their concerns. Professors and teachers encourage their students to engage in discussion and voice their opinions.

   a. Since you started studying English, have you noticed U.S. citizens being vocal?

   b. What kinds of issues were they addressing?

   c. In your opinion, is it always acceptable to be vocal?

   d. Have you ever been vocal about an issue? What was it? What did you say about it and to whom?

   e. List some words that are related to *vocal*.

3. When a country has increasing numbers of people living in large cities, the country is becoming **urbanized**. The United States experienced urbanization at the turn of the 20th century. Since World War II, housing and businesses began to move rapidly into suburbs, often leaving the cities to decay. Today, efforts at renewing urban centers are common in large metropolitan areas. Worldwide, many developing nations are beginning to experience rapid urbanization.

   a. What effects of urbanization and suburbanization have you seen or heard about in the U.S. today?

   b. Do you prefer to live in a large city or a smaller town? Why?

   c. What are some advantages of living in a large city? What are some problems?

   d. List some words that are related to *urbanization*.

4. Newspaper reporters (called *the press*) who exposed crime and other problems at the turn of the century were called **muckrakers**. *Muck* is the dirt and waste found in animal stalls. The stories created by the journalists stopped many unethical practices in U.S. American businesses. However, the business owners often felt that the reporters took away their right to run their businesses without interference. The U.S. Constitution guarantees freedom of the press, so newspapers can publish stories without the government's approval.

   a. Do you think that the U.S. press should have the right to print anything it chooses?

   b. What are the benefits and problems of such a system?

   c. Do you know of places where the press is not free to publish what it chooses?

   d. What do you think about the idea of media freedom?

   e. List some words that are related to *muckrakers*.

Before Reading: Making Predictions

Making predictions (whether you are right or wrong) is a good step toward better reading in any language. Without looking ahead at the reading, list some ideas you think will be included in the reading based on the title and general topic.

_____

_____

_____

_____

_____

_____

Reading: The U.S. at the Beginning of the 20th Century

At the dawn of the 20th century, the United States was still a growing country with only 46 of its current 50 states. A large part of this growth was a result of people seeking a new life. Ellis Island in New York was receiving one hundred immigrants per hour, most of whom headed for rapidly growing cities such as New York City (3.4 million) and Chicago (1.6 million). Whereas in the 19th century, U.S. Americans had mostly lived in rural areas and worked in **agriculture**, they also began to **flock** to the cities at the beginning of the 20th century. There, they joined immigrant populations working in large factories and creating a consumer market for all the goods being produced there. New technology expanded rapidly as automobiles began to replace horses on American streets and over a million people had telephones. Life and work in the city was an improvement in the standard of living for many poor and rural families.

Industry (oil on canvas) by Arthur Durston. This painting depicted the long hours of workers in the Industrial Era. (Courtesy Smithsonian American Art Museum.)

However, the rapid growth, **industrialization,** and capitalism that created possibilities also brought problems: crowded cities, poor housing conditions, low **wages** for a hard day's work, and long days. Many workers were **exploited** by their employers—especially those who had no say about their work such as women, children, and immigrants. At that time, there were no laws regulating child labor, and although social activist

Workers in the Canton Glass Works in Marion, Indiana, in the early 1900s. (Courtesy Library of Congress.)

leaders such as Mother Jones* were trying to make sure that they spent their days in school, many young American children worked 12-hour days doing dangerous jobs in dirty factories. Profit became more important than the safety of the workers, and **monopolies** grew large and powerful. When laws to protect workers were passed, rich factory owners **bribed** officials to look the other way when they found problems. A growing social movement in the middle class began to organize in **opposition** to these problems. Awareness was brought about largely by the press. Reporters (often called "**muckrakers**") wrote newspaper stories about children working in the factories. A famous author, Upton Sinclair, wrote *The Jungle* in 1906. The novel **exposed** the dirty conditions of a Chicago meat-packing factory where his characters, an immigrant family from Lithuania, worked. The book influenced the government to eventually pass the *Pure Food and Drug Act* to protect U.S. citizens from unsafe food.

Due to the harsh working conditions, many people turned to drinking. Seeing many social and family problems caused by the overuse of alcohol, women's groups began to focus their efforts on making it illegal. The *Prohibition Act* of 1919 is a **constitutional amendment** that made producing, selling, or drinking alcohol illegal in every U.S. state. The Eighteenth Amendment was supported by many industrial and

---

*Mother Jones: Mary Harris Jones was an important person in the fight for workers' rights and against child labor.

A suffragist works to win the vote for women, 1914. (Courtesy Library of Congress.)

religious leaders, who thought that it would help U.S. Americans to be more productive at work, family-oriented at home, and **moral** in society. However, it was expensive and difficult to enforce the law, and many people began to brew alcohol in their own homes, creating unsafe drinks that sometimes caused illness and even death. Illegal alcohol production and sales became big **underground** business for gangsters such as Al Capone. Because of the cost and the dangers of private alcohol man-ufacturing, the Eighteenth Amendment was **repealed** fourteen years later and replaced with the Twenty-First Amendment, which made the production and sales of alcohol in the U.S. legal again.

Having found their voices in the public realm, women began to organize around the issue of universal **suffrage**. The symbolic birthplace of the women's suffrage move-ment was at an 1848 women's conference at Seneca Falls, New York. Elizabeth Cady Stanton and Susan B. Anthony led the movement during the early 1900s and it contin-ued to grow during the Prohibition era. Although some women were legally able to vote in a few western states, the Nineteenth Amendment, the *Suffrage Act* of 1919, gave U.S. women the right to vote nationwide. (In 1971, the Twenty-Sixth Amendment set the voting age at eighteen for all **eligible** citizens.)

The vision and hard work of immigrants and native-born U.S. Americans com-bined with the dedication of journalists and social workers caused many large, positive, wide-scale changes in both public and private life during the first two decades of the 20th century.

Responding to Information about the Rise of Large Industry and a Cry for Social Reform

Complete these activities.

1. Make a list of the ideas from the reading that are most important to you. How do these ideas affect you or your life?

_____

_____

_____

_____

_____

_____

2. Choose one idea from your list, and write a few notes about it here. Then write a paragraph about it on a separate sheet of paper. How does it relate to your personal life? Describe the person or event in detail.

_____

_____

_____

_____

_____

_____

Understanding the Reading: Comprehension Check

Look at each topic, and match it to the group of people that it is most closely related to according to the reading. The first one has been done for you.

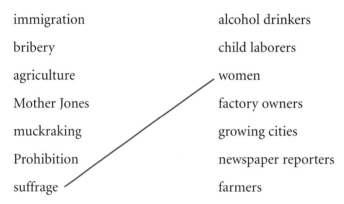

immigration   alcohol drinkers

bribery   child laborers

agriculture   women

Mother Jones   factory owners

muckraking   growing cities

Prohibition   newspaper reporters

suffrage   farmers

Talking about Immigration and Employment

The novel mentioned in the reading, *The Jungle*, is about an immigrant family's experience adjusting to life in the U.S. while working in a large Chicago factory. The novel shows how the quality of life in some communities is heavily influenced by the type of employers who are dominant in the area.

Before reading three paragraphs from Upton Sinclair's novel, conduct a mini-interview with a partner. Learn about employment in his or her family's home country. Ask about:

1. your partner's country, region, and hometown

2. the area's largest employer

3. the impact of that employer on the community

4. the importance of the company to the city or region

5. the treatment of workers by that company or industry

6. the personal experiences with that employer/industry, if any

Looking at a Novel: *The Jungle* by Upton Sinclair

The Jungle was written by Upton Sinclair and published in 1906. It is the story of an immigrant named Jurgis, who comes from Lithuania to seek fortune for himself and his family in the United States. Jurgis and his family settle in Chicago and begin to work in a meat factory. This story exposed the unsanitary conditions of the early 20th century food industry in the United States, and it showed the hard lifestyle of the working class. The novel led to many reforms such as the *Pure Food and Drug Act* and laws to protect children from working in factories. Sinclair dedicated the book "To the workingmen of America."

Read these passages from *The Jungle.* Some unfamiliar words are explained for you in brackets [ ].

The first passage is from the beginning of the story when Jurgis and his family are new to the United States. Jurgis and Ona are engaged to be married. With them were several aunts and uncles who brought their children. Some of the relatives pay rent to Jurgis. Jurgis and several adult members of the family have just found jobs at the factory in Packingtown—the stockyards of Chicago.

Better luck than this could hardly be hoped for; there was only one of them left to seek a place. Jurgis was determined [*had decided*] that Teta Elzbieta should stay at home to keep house, and that Ona should help her. He would not have Ona working—he was not that sort of man, he said, and she was not that sort of woman. It would be a strange thing if a man like him could not support the family, with the help of the board [*rent money*] of Jonas and Marija. He would not even hear of letting the children go to work—there were schools here in America for children, Jurgis had heard, to which they could go for nothing. That the priest would object to these schools was something of which he had as yet no idea, and for the present his mind was made up that the children of Teta Elzbieta should have as fair a chance as any other children. The oldest of them, little Stanislovas, was but thirteen, and small for his age at that, and while the oldest son of Szedvillas was only twelve, and had worked for over a year at Jones', Jurgis would have it that Stanislovas should learn to speak English, and grow up to be a skilled man. (pp. 47–48)

The second passage is from the middle of the story, after the family members have found out that they were cheated when they bought a home. They cannot afford to pay the interest on their mortgage loan, so Ona pays a bribe to the factory boss and gets a job packing hams in tin cans. Then Jurgis sends his 14-year-old nephew Stanislovas to the city to look for work.

> And so, after little Stanislovas had stood gazing timidly [*scared*] about him for a few minutes, a man approached him and asked what he wanted, to which Stanislovas said "Job." Then the man said, "How old?" and Stanislovas answered "Sixtin." Once or twice every year a state inspector would come wandering through the packing plants, asking a child here and there how old he was; and so the packers were very careful to comply with [*follow*] the law, which cost them as much trouble as was now involved in taking the document [*birth certificate or proof of age*] from the boy, and glancing [*looking quickly and not carefully*] at it, and then sending it to the office to be filed away. Then he set someone else at a different job and showed the lad how to place a lard can every time the empty arm of the remorseless [*never stopping*] machine came to him; and so was decided the place in the universe of little Stanislovas, and his destiny to the end of his days. Hour after hour, day after day, year after year, it was fated that he should stand upon a certain square foot of floor from seven in the morning until noon, and again from half-past twelve till half-past five, making never a motion and thinking never a thought, save for [*except for*] the setting of the lard cans. In the summer the stench [*bad smell*] of the warm lard would be nauseating [*making somebody sick to the stomach*], and in the winter the cans would all but freeze to his naked little fingers in the unheated cellar. Half the year it would be dark as night when he went in to work, and dark as night again when he came out, and so he would never know what the sun looked like on weekdays. And for this, at the end of the week, he would carry home three dollars to his family, being his pay at the rate of five cents per hour. . . . " (pp. 75–76)

The final passage is from the end of the novel. The people who were paying rent moved out, cutting the family's income by one-third. The grandfather and a child have died, and the whole family is fighting various problems. Most of the family members have lost their physically demanding first jobs because of job-related injuries and illness and have been forced to take lower-paying, more difficult jobs in other factories or departments to survive.

They were beaten; they had lost the game, they were swept aside. It was not less tragic because it was so sordid [*extremely base, dirty, and morally depressing*], because it had to do with wages and grocery bills and rents. They had dreamed of freedom; of a chance to look about them and learn something; to be decent and clean; to see their child grow up to be strong. And now it was all gone—it never would be! . . . Jurgis, being a man, had troubles of his own. There was another specter [*disturbing or haunting image; a ghost*] following him. He had never spoken of it, nor would he allow anyone else to speak of it—he had never acknowledged it [*admitted it to*] himself. Yet the battle with it took all manhood he had—and once or twice, alas, a little more. Jurgis had discovered drink [*alcohol*]. (p. 138)

LANGUAGE FOCUS: Using Descriptive Language

The characters in the novel experience increased stress and their lives change a lot from the beginning of the story to the end. As their lives change, so do their attitudes. Based on the novel excerpts that you read, make a list of as many adjectives as you can think of to describe Jurgis and his family at the beginning of the story, the middle of the story, and the end of the story.

Beginning of the Story	Middle of the Story	End of the Story
pleased		
excited		

Discuss your adjective lists with a partner. Use the adjectives to describe what happens to Jurgis in the end. Talk about Ona and Stanislovas. How do you think they each turn out? What kinds of attitudes and feelings do they develop?

1. Adjectives and short phrases can be used to create a poem of sorts about the information you have. For example, this poem is about Packingtown and uses the letters of the name *Packingtown* as the first letters of adjectives or short phrases that describe information from the novel.

   P utrid
   A wful
   C old
   K illing animals
   I n a
   N ever-ending assembly line
   G ut shoveling Jurgis
   T ries to keep up
   O nly to be
   W orked to death
   N o more money; No more hope

Use adjectives or phrases to make a similar poem with the first letters of words such as *factory, wages, monopoly, voting,* etc. Use any vocabulary words from the list in the unit, or use any word you think is connected to the information in this unit.

_____

_____

_____

_____

_____

_____

2. When people change their attitude about something, it is often because they see the situation in a new way. What do you think Jurgis and his family realized about their situation? Describe in writing how you think Jurgis felt when that happened.

_____

_____

_____

_____

3. Have you ever seen a situation in a new way and then changed your attitude? Write a descriptive paragraph about what happened. Describe the setting (where it happened and how things looked, smelled, sounded, etc.), what ideas led to the change, and how things in your life changed.

_____

_____

_____

_____

_____

_____

Speaking about Your Own Life Changes: Culture Shock

Upton Sinclair wrote *The Jungle* to help people in the United States realize that the wealth of large industry was only an appearance—that, in reality, many people worked in terrible conditions in order to make a few people wealthy. Although Sinclair's novel was intended mainly to expose the problems of immigrant workers and the uncontrolled pursuit to capitalism, another major theme of *The Jungle* was the immigrant experience and the family's recognition that life in the United States was not what they thought it would be.

When people move to a new country, it is common for them to experience culture shock. These same feelings can be triggered by moving to a new community, buying a house, getting married, having a child, going back to school, or experiencing any large life change. People tend to imagine an experience will be a certain way, only to find out that it is not that way. When this kind of realization occurs, it is called *disillusionment*. Disillusionment is the second stage of "culture shock."

Read descriptions of each stage in the process.

Stage	Symptoms
Honeymoon Stage	excitement, euphoria, feelings of control and confidence in the new country or situation
Disillusionment	frustration and anger, dislike of the new things that were once exciting, wanting to be with people from your own country or community, physical symptoms such as irritability or not sleeping
Culture Stress	some problems are solved and some are not, differences become less problematic, feelings of belonging to both the familiar and unfamiliar communities but not completely to either
Assimilation	acceptance of new culture or situation and self-confidence

1. Are you experiencing or have you ever experienced any of these stages of culture shock? Describe one.

   _____

   _____

   _____

2. Talk about culture shock with a partner. Has your partner experienced it? Is he or she experiencing it now? What ideas do you have about coping with culture shock or helping another person cope with it?

   _____

   _____

LANGUAGE FOCUS: Using Suggestion Phrases

Suggestions are ideas, advice, or proposals. For example, people suggest ways to accomplish tasks. There are several words or phrases that are used before making a suggestion. Some are stronger than others. Work with your instructor and classmates to rewrite these suggestion phrases in order from the least strong to the most strong. If you think two phrases are equal, write them next to each other. Add any other words or phrases you can think of.

	Least Strong
It's a good idea to	
Let's	
Why don't you	
You might want to	
You ought to	
You could	
You should	
	Most Strong

1. What other phrases did you add?

   _____

   _____

   _____

A note about sociolinguistic and appropriate English: In U.S. American culture, the phrase *you must* crosses the boundary line of suggestion. U.S. American English speakers understand *you must* as a soft command. *You must* should never be used when making a suggestion among equals or with a person of higher status. Please remove *you must* from your list of suggestion phrases if you added it.

2. Practice with classmates by using appropriate suggestion phrases to suggest that they do these things to overcome culture shock.

- eat nutritious food

- exercise regularly

- get enough sleep

- join an international student club or civic organization

- keep an open mind and note new things that they like about the new situation as well as the things that they dislike

- keep in contact with friends and family

- keep up on events at home via newspapers or the Internet

- network with a social, religious, or linguistic community

- understand that learning to adapt to a new culture or life event is a process and will not happen overnight

- understand that adapting to a new culture or life event does not mean that prior experiences will become less valid

3. What other suggestions do you have, based on your personal experience?

_____

_____

_____

LINK TO TODAY: Fast Food—Eating on the Go

America is a nation on the go, and a good majority of people eat at a fast food restaurant at least once during the week. In the face of a national obesity problem, some national food chains have begun to make healthier products and market them to people who want to live a healthier lifestyle. They have started using organic fruits and vegetables, using hormone-free milk and chicken, and purchasing antibiotic-free beef. However, other chains have taken the opposite approach by supersizing and offering products with increasing amounts of fat, sodium, and sugar. In his popular book and movie *Fast Food Nation* (first published in 2002), investigative journalist Eric Schlosser painted a comprehensive picture of the fast food industry and its effects on farmers, ranchers, workers, and consumers.

"In many respects, the fast food industry embodies the best and the worst of American capitalism at the start of the twenty-first century—its constant stream of new products and innovations, its widening gulf between rich and poor. The industrialization of the restaurant kitchen has enabled the fast food chains to rely upon a low-paid and unskilled workforce. While a handful of workers manage to rise up the corporate ladder, the vast majority lack full-time employment, receive no benefits, learn few skills, exercise little control over their workplace, quit after a few months, and float from job to job. The restaurant industry is now America's largest private employer, and it pays some of the lowest wages. During the economic boom of the 1990s, when many American workers enjoyed their first pay raises in a generation, the real value of wages in the restaurant industry continued to fall. The roughly 3.5 million fast food workers are by far the largest group of minimum wage earners in the United States. The only Americans who consistently earn a lower hourly wage are migrant farm workers." (p. 6)

Fast Facts

Americans spend more money on fast food than on higher education, personal computers, computer software, or new cars. They spend more on fast food than on movies, books, magazines, newspapers, videos, and recorded music—combined.[1]

- In April 2011, the U.S. governement proposed guidelines that could lead to major changes in how the food industry in general advertises food, such as cereal and soda, and restaurant meals to children.[2]

- In 2010, the San Francisco Board of Supervisors passed a law banning city restaurants from including toys with children's meals that contained too much fat/sodium/sugar. The city mayor threatened to veto the controversial legislation.[3]

- A study sponsored by the Centers for Disease Control published in 2010 found that racial/ethnic minority communities in urban Los Angeles are at high risk of obesity and diabetes because their access to stores selling affordable, nutritious food was too limited.[4]

- The U.S. Bureau of Labor Statistics has estimated that there will be 3,670,400 people employed as fast food counter workers by the year 2018. Worldwide, the number will be much higher.[5]

- A study published in the *Global Economy Journal* in 2007 found that fast food franchises bring positive economic growth to mid-range and developing economies. They offer management training, entrepreneurship, revenue for local suppliers, and improvements in customer service standards.[6]

---

[1] Schlosser, Eric. (2002). *Fast Food Nation: The dark side of the all-American meal.* Harper Collins: New York.

[2] Newman, William. (2011). U.S. seeks new limits on food ads for children. *The New York Times.* www.nytimes.com/2011/04/29/business/29label.html.

[3] McKinley, Jesse. (2010) *Citing Obesity of Children, County Bans Fast-Food Toys.* www.nytimes.com/2010/04/28/business/28mcdonalds.html.

[4] Azuma A.M., Gilliland, S., Vallianatos, M., Gottlieb, R. (2010). Food access, availability, and affordability in 3 Los Angeles communities, Project CAFE, 2004–2006. *Prevention of Chronic Disease,* 7(2). www.cdc.gov/pcd/issues/2010/mar/08_0232.htm.

[5] *U. S. Bureau of Labor and Statistics Occupational Outlook Handbook.* (2010–11 Edition). www.bls.gov/oco/ocos162.htm.

[6] Tschoegl, Adrian E. (2007). "McDonald's—Much Maligned, But an Engine of Economic Development." *Global Economy Journal* 7(4): 1–16. www.bepress.com/gej/vol7/iss4/5/.

Find and read two newspaper, magazine, or Internet articles, one with positive aspects of fast food and one detailing the negative aspects. Summarize each article. Then write a short pargraph about your personal conclusions.

positive aspects of fast food

_____

_____

_____

_____

negative aspects of fast food

_____

_____

_____

_____

my personal conclusions about fast food in the United States

_____

_____

_____

_____

Putting It All Together

With each unit, you will learn more and more new information about U.S. culture and history. It is important to take some time to process new information. Reflect, and then write your ideas about these questions. Then discuss them in a group.

1. What surprised me most about the U.S. in the early part of the 20th century?

   _____

   _____

2. What does this information help me to understand about modern U.S. American life?

   _____

   _____

3. Does this information change my opinions about U.S. American values and attitudes? How?

   _____

   _____

4. Can people in other countries learn something from the lessons the U.S. learned from Prohibition and the labor/social reform era? If so, what?

   _____

   _____

5. What positive changes can countries make regarding labor/social reform for workers?

   _____

   _____

6. What aspects of the Prohibition movement are similar to San Francisco's proposed laws about children's meals at fast food restaurants?

   _____

   _____

7. What programs or policies would make transitioning to a new place easier for newcomers and immigrants in terms of working, voting, etc.?

   _____

   _____

2 The U.S. between World Wars

The Roaring Twenties, Black Tuesday, and Beyond

Representative T. S. McMillan of Charleston, SC, with flappers who are doing the Charleston during the 1920s. (Photo by National Photo Co., Courtesy Library of Congress.)

Many changes occurred in the United States during the first two decades of the 20th century. Most of that change was for the better, but this unit focuses on a time of liberation and growth that led to a financial crisis.

Net Surfers

To learn more about the time period covered in this unit, search for these names, words, and phrases on the Internet.

all about jazz	the 1920s experience
isolationism	Great Outdoor Recreation Pages
Civilian Conservation Corps	National Park Service
the Jazz Age	Prohibition
Documenting America portfolios (1930s)	the Roaring Twenties
jazz biographies	the history of jazz music
the history of the Dust Bowl	Social Security Administration

Presidential Suite

Woodrow Wilson (D) 1913–1921
Warren G. Harding (R) 1921–1923
Calvin Coolidge (R) 1923–1929
Herbert C. Hoover (R) 1929–1933
Franklin Delano Roosevelt (D) 1933–1945

Music Box

"Are You Makin' Any Money?"—
Chick Bullock and His Levee Loungers (1933)
"Brother, Can You Spare a Dime?"—Rudy Vallee (1932)
"Gloomy Sunday"—Billie Holiday (1941)
"Happy Days Are Here Again"—Casa Loma Orchestra (1929)
"Headin' For Better Times"—Ted Lewis and His Band (1931)
"It Don't Mean a Thing (If It Ain't Got That Swing)"—
Duke Ellington and His Orchestra (1932)
"There's a New Day Comin'"—Ted Lewis and His Band (1933)
"We Sure Got Hard Times Now"—Barbecue Bob (1930)

On TV

The Waltons

At the Movies

The Grapes of Wrath (adapted from the novel)
Of Mice and Men (adapted from the novel)

Preparing to Read about the Roaring Twenties, Black Tuesday, and Beyond

Write some thoughts about these topics, and then discuss them with your classmates.

1. the stock market and investing

   a. Is it a good idea to risk money on the stock market? _____

   b. What are the best and worst stocks to invest in? _____

   _____

2. going to war

   a. What wars has your family's home country been involved in? _____

   _____

   b. How is war viewed in that country? Is it accepted publicly? _____

   _____

   c. What is your viewpoint on war? Is it sometimes necessary or to be avoided at all costs? _____

   _____

3. wealth and poverty

   a. What is daily life like for people in your family's home country?

   _____

   _____

   b. What does the government there do to help people with less money?

   _____

   _____

Learning New Vocabulary about the U.S. between World Wars

Although this is a long list of words to learn, these words will be helpful to understanding the reading. Review the vocabulary and definitions, and refer to this list as needed.

advocate (**n**) supporter; somebody who promotes something

conservation (**n**) the act of protecting or setting something aside

drought (**n**) an extended period without rain during which no crops can grow

flapper (**n**) name for a modern woman in the 1920s

Great Depression (**n**) a time of economic problems in the U.S. between 1929–1941

infrastructure (**n**) system of public works

isolationism (**n**) belief in only wanting to deal with one's own existence

leadership (**n**) ability to lead or be in charge of something

poverty (**n**) the state of not having enough money; being poor

prosperity (**n**) wealth or economic well-being

reform (**n**) change in laws

renaissance (**n**) a rebirth

self-confidence (**n**) strong belief in oneself

topsoil (**n**) the top layer of soil rich in nutrients and good for plants

to cope (**v**) to deal with; to handle

to sweep (**v**) to take over or spread from one area to another

to wipe out (**v**) to completely destroy; to no longer exist

desperate (**adj**) having great need

neutral (**adj**) not taking sides

progressive (**adj**) modern or forward thinking

sufficient (**adj**) enough

initially (**adv**) at first

Talking about New Words and Concepts

Take some time to think and talk about new ideas associated with the vocabulary. Then use your understanding of the new vocabulary to discuss each set of questions with a partner.

1. When a country makes an effort to protect its natural resources, it is referred to as an act of **conservation**. The U.S. has a long tradition of preserving places of natural beauty and shielding them from the negative effects of commercial, for-profit development. The United States' first national park, Yellowstone, was set aside in 1879.

   a. What effects of conservation do you see today in U.S. society?

   b. Do you think this trend will continue in the future, or do you see it declining?

   c. How do you think people in other countries view U.S. conservation efforts?

   d. What do you think other countries should do to promote conservation efforts?

   e. List some words that are related to *conservation.*

2. When a country does not want to get involved in the problems of other countries and instead prefers to concentrate on internal issues, it is said to be in a phase of **isolationism**. The United States has gone through various stages of isolationism, even though many believe that the United States acts as the "police officer to the world."

   a. Can you think of a specific crisis that the U.S. chose not to get involved in?

   b. Why do you think the United States chose not to get involved?

   c. What countries today have an isolationist mentality?

   d. Is a country's isolationist mentality an advantage or a disadvantage?

   e. Is it possible for one country to choose only to deal with its own problems in a global society?

   f. List some words that are related to *isolationism.*

3. When something experiences a rebirth in society, it is said to be undergoing a **renaissance**. For example, in the United States today, people talk of an urban renaissance, meaning that the large cities are being reborn after a long period of decay. Certain kinds of literature, music, or art also experience a renaissance at various time periods. History shows us that things tend to be reborn about every 30 years. Since the recent economic turndown, values and attitudes similar to those during the **Great Depression**—such as saving money, practicing thrift, and reusing things—have become trendy and fashionable. "Down home" cooking and simple food have become popular fare in restaurants.

   a. Is there something in your community that is experiencing a renaissance? If so, what?

   b. Why do you think old things become popular again with younger generations?

   c. List some words that are related to *renaissance*.

4. When someone is a strong supporter of something, we say that he or she is an **advocate**. If you look closely at the word *advocate,* you will notice that it contains the stem *voc,* which is also a root of *voice* and *vocal.* Therefore, the word *advocate* has to do with somebody who uses his or her voice or speaks up for something and promotes it publicly.

   a. Are you an advocate for something? If so, what?

   b. How do you promote it?

   c. What is the result of your being an advocate for something?

   d. Has your effort been successful?

   e. List some words that are related to *advocate*.

5. When someone takes the responsibility of being in charge of something, we say that he or she has assumed a **leadership** role.

   a. Have you ever taken a leadership role in an activity or in your community?

   b. Do you like or dislike being a leader? For what reason(s)?

   c. How acceptable is it for women to take leadership positions in your community? Young people?

   d. List some words that are related to *leadership*.

Before Reading: Making Predictions

Making predictions about a reading is beneficial to language learning because it activates your prior knowledge and gets you thinking about the topic in advance. This makes comprehension easier.

In pairs or in a small group, review the discussion you had with your classmates about investing, war, and poverty and the other new words you learned (see pages 30 and 31–32). Based on this discussion, make a list of five ideas you think will be discussed in the next reading passage.

1. _____

2. _____

3. _____

4. _____

5. _____

Compare your list with the lists of two other students. Which ideas are similar? Which are different? Are there any ideas from your classmates that make you think you might like to change your ideas? If so, list them here.

_____

_____

_____

_____

_____

_____

Reading: The U.S. between World Wars

The first two decades of 20th century U.S. history revolved largely around internal migration to the cities and **reforms** to working and living conditions. The focus on internal policy was evident in President Woodrow Wilson's creation of the National Parks Service in 1916 to protect an expanding network of what has grown today to include 58 parks. However, this internal focus was interrupted when the U.S. unexpectedly found itself involved in a European war. Wilson, who was an **advocate** of peace and neutrality, was determined to keep his country out of the conflict and managed to maintain a **neutral** stance for three years. However, in 1917 he asked Congress to declare war on Germany as the result of repeated attacks on U.S. and British cargo ships in the Atlantic Ocean and, finally, the sinking of a British passenger ship, the *Lusitania*. The American public was **initially** not supportive of the war, and the all-volunteer Army was not **sufficient**. This led to the creation of the Selective Service whereby all men of a certain age were forced to register with the military. A set number of troops were sent "over there" to battle the Germans. After the victory, Wilson proposed the intergovernmental peacekeeping organization that later became the United Nations.

President Wilson addresses Congress regarding U.S. involvement in World War I, February 3, 1917. (Courtesy DoD Visual Information Record Center.)

The great jazz musician Duke Ellington. (Courtesy DoD Visual Information Record Center.)

Returning soldiers came back to a rapidly expanding economy and a nation that was growing more self-confident while increasingly committing itself to **isolationism** and giving attention to its own internal affairs. The 1920s era of fun-loving **prosperity** was known as the Roaring Twenties.

During these ten years, the nation's wealth doubled, and the salary of the average worker rose by 10 percent, partly due to the expanding economy and partly due to the positive effect of new labor laws. The dollar became strong, people began to invest in corporate life, and the New York stock market soared. Theater, literature, and art experienced a **renaissance,** and movies were born. Jazz, a new form of music from New Orleans, **swept** the country with artists such as Duke Ellington and Louis Armstrong playing the music that the young loved despite (and probably because of) their parents' dissatisfaction. Women especially enjoyed a new **self-confidence** gained from their leadership in reform movements and participation in the suffrage movement for voting rights. Their **progressive** attitudes became visible when they began to flaunt short "bobbed" hair, wear shorter skirts (no longer floor length), and dance in public. Some of the more daring ones were known to drink, smoke, and gamble. These females became known as "**flappers**"—perhaps because of the flapping sound that their fringed

A young man copes with the Great Depression. (Courtesy Library of Congress.)

and heavily beaded dresses made when dancing—and were viewed as immoral for their fun-loving public behavior by more conservative members of society.

Just as it seemed that the good times could go on forever, America's free, fun-loving, and risk-taking lifestyle came to an end when the stock market crashed on October 24, 1929, a day known as "Black Tuesday." Many people's savings were **wiped out** overnight, and banks were forced to close in the years to follow. The economic crisis was not confined to Wall Street*, however, as farms and businesses all over the country failed and unemployment increased. In addition to these problems, parts of the Midwest and the Southwest were also experiencing a severe **drought** that made it impossible to grow crops. Much of the **topsoil** dried, cracked, and blew away in a natural disaster that came to be called the Dust Bowl, portrayed by the author John Steinbeck in one of his novels. Thus, by the early 1930s, about one-quarter of the U.S. population was unemployed and **coping** with an economic crisis known as the Great Depression.

Poverty in the United States could be seen in the cardboard and wood scrap houses outside of cities. These shanties were called "Hoovervilles"—named after the president at that time, Herbert Hoover. In the cities, thousands stood in line daily for a meal of

---

***Wall Street:** the financial district in New York City, and often all U.S. financial activities.

A plaque shows the location of a WPA hiking trail project, Tucson, Arizona.

soup and bread. Many **desperate** Midwestern farm families migrated across the country, heading to the West Coast in search of agricultural work and the ability to grow their own food in fertile soil again.

Noting that he saw one-third of a nation in poverty and promising U.S. Americans a "New Deal" and a chicken in every pot, Franklin D. Roosevelt (FDR) was elected president in 1932. Roosevelt set to work, and within the first 100 days of his presidency, Congress had approved a number of emergency projects to help U.S. citizens cope with the Depression. One of the most important was the Works Progress Administration (WPA), which employed millions of people while improving roads, dams, sidewalks, and schools. These projects improved the country's **infrastructure.** In addition, many forest **conservation** projects, hiking trails, and national park beautification projects came about because of the Civilian Conservation Corps (CCC). Artists, authors, playwrights, photographers, and storytellers went to work depicting the crisis and recording people's stories. One of the most well known was photographer Dorothea Lange, whose pictures came to represent the era in the minds of many. These programs continued to provide work and dignity to a large number of Americans until the U.S. was forced once again to enter a world war—this time against Japan and Germany.

Responding to Information about the Roaring Twenties, Black Tuesday, and Beyond

Complete these activities.

1. Complete the summary chart of the main ideas from the reading, what they remind you of, and what connection you make between them and what you know about U.S. American life.

Main Ideas	Reminds Me of	Connection to U.S. American Life

2. Choose what you think is the most important main idea from your list, and write a few notes about it here. Then write a paragraph about it on a separate piece of paper. Describe how it is important to you personally. Describe how you connect it to your knowledge of U.S. American life or U.S. American citizens.

_____

_____

_____

Understanding the Reading: Comprehension Check

Without looking back at the reading, use your new understanding and knowledge to circle the best word or phase for the sentence.

Even though the United States did not want to, it became involved in

World War I because of German attacks on British and American

(war/passenger) ships. After the war, the United States decided to

focus on (itself/other countries). The 1920s were a (depressing/

wild) time. People had (fun/problems). New (dances and movies/

sports and radios) entertained people. Women became more (progressive/

conservative). Older people (celebrated/rejected) the new ways.

When the stock market crashed, people (panicked/rejoiced)

because they were (rich/ruined). The Great Depression caused

(unemployment and homelessness/an economic boom and security).

President Franklin Delano Roosevelt promised to (help Americans/

fight the Germans). The New Deal provided U.S. Americans with

(problems and fear/jobs and hope).

Check your answers with your classmates and instructor. Go back and read the text again. Try to focus on reading more carefully to understand any incorrect answers.

Viewing WPA Photography

During the Great Depression, as many as one-third of U.S. Americans were living in poverty. The WPA was created to put as many people to work as possible. Projects were designed to be large and/or elaborate so that many people could work on them and receive a paycheck. While many people were put to work constructing large buildings, dams, and projects, others set to work on beautification efforts such as public sculptures, murals, and paintings. Some people felt that these projects were a waste of time, but if you look carefully when you visit the United States, you will find that many still exist, beautifying public buildings and open spaces.

A large group of artists that included playwrights, painters, musicians, writers, and photographers was also put to work, creating plays and songs for much needed free, public entertainment. Others documented the life histories of the U.S. American population through word and film. One such project, entitled "One Third of a Nation" by photographers Arnold Eagle and David Robbins, documented the Great Depression via photography. Another featured the photographs of Dorothea Lange, a well-known Depression-era photographer. Read this passage in which Lange described taking her iconic photo of a migrant mother.

> I saw and approached the hungry and desperate mother, as if drawn by a magnet. I do not remember how I explained my presence or my camera to her, but I do remember she asked me no questions. I made five exposures, working closer and closer from the same direction. I did not ask her name or her history. She told me her age, that she was thirty-two. She said that they had been living on frozen vegetables from the surrounding fields, and birds that the children killed. She had just sold the tires from her car to buy food.

Photo of a migrant mother by Dorothea Lange. (Courtesy Library of Congress.)

A woman and her children face the Great Depression. Photo by Dorothea Lange. (Courtesy Library of Congress.)

Mother and Boy at Table. Slum conditions in the congested East Side and Charles districts of New York City are recorded in a group "One Third of a Nation," 1938. (WPA Photo. Courtesy U.S. National Archives and Records Administration.)

Talking about the Photographs

Look at the three photos on page 41, and answer the questions according to your own observations and interpretations.

	Woman and Children	Mother and Boy	Migrant Mother at Table
What do you think is happening in the photograph?			
What is the mood of the people?			
What do you think the people do for a living?			
Do you think the people are related to each other? If so, how?			
What is similar in all the photos?			
What is different in each photo?			
What do you think the photographer's message is?			

Use the answers to these questions and your creativity to write a story about the people in the photos. You may use the photos in any sequence you wish, but make sure that each photograph illustrates part of your story. Be creative.

LANGUAGE FOCUS: Using Backchanneling Strategies to Show Interest in Speaker Narratives

When native speakers of American English want to show interest in a narrative or other information given by another speaker, they often use a strategy called *backchanneling*. This is verbal and non-verbal feedback that shows interest and emotions, telling the speaker that the listeners are paying attention and interested in hearing him/her continue. U.S. English speakers rely on this feedback, and if they don't get it, they may stop communicating. If a listener remains completely silent, it may confuse the speaker and cause him/her to stop talking. A good rule of thumb when listening to English speakers is a nod or verbal acknowledgment such as *mmmm* or *uh-huh* for every three or four sentences spoken. Look at this list of words and phrases commonly used for backchanneling and their functions.

Word or Phrase	Function
Uh-huh. *Mmmmm.* *(Nodding head up and down.)*	Signal listening and the listener's willingness to have the speaker continue without interruption.
I see. *Ahhhh.* *And then?*	Signal listening for content and the wish for more information.
Oh? *Oh, really?* *Oh, yeah?* *Wow!*	Signal mild surprise and the wish for the speaker to continue giving information. Can also signal a little doubt, usually with facial expressions such as wrinkled eyebrows.
Ah-hah!	Signals wished-for or key piece of information.
Sure.	Signals general agreement with the speaker's viewpoints and a supportive stance.
No way!	Signals disagreement. Can also signal strong surprise but general agreement with speaker's viewpoint.
No. *Uh-uh.*	Signal disagreement.
All right.	Signals agreement, usually about plans, or approval (stress on *right*).
Sounds great!	Signals strong agreement, usually about plans.
Awwww.	Signals mild dismay or sympathy.
Gee, I don't know.	Signals inability to respond to information but not disagreement
Oh, sorry. *Sorry, go on.* *Sorry, you were saying?*	Signal improper interruption on the listener's wish to apologize and let the speaker continue.

1. What kind of non-verbal feedback can be used for each function?

   _____

   _____

2. Work in groups of three. Assign roles. One person is the storyteller, one person is the listener, and one person is the observer. The storyteller tells the listener the story he/she wrote about the photos. The listener practices using appropriate backchanneling strategies. The observer should not speak at all, but should note the backchanneling phrases used and whether they were effective. The observer shares his/her notes with the storyteller and listener, and the group discusses the experience. Continue until each person in the group has had a turn to be the storyteller, the listener, and the observer.

Bear Market/Bull Market—The New York Stock Exchange

- The New York Stock Exchange (NYSE) operates financial markets and manages trading. As of 2007, it is a combination of the NYSE and Euronext, making it the first international exchange operator since it has offices in Europe and the United States. The offices trade products such as stocks in the market.

- The Dow Jones Industrial Average (DJIA) is based on a group of 30 industrial companies (excluding transportation and utilities) with a history of successful growth and wide investor interest.

- The NYSE Composite Index tracks the price movements of all common stocks listed on the New York Stock Exchange.

- The S&P 500 Composite Stock Price Index is a weighted index of 500 stocks that represent leading companies in the U.S. economy.

- The Wilshire 5000 Total Market Index measures the entire U.S. stock market.

- The Russell 2000® Index measures the performance of the 2,000 smallest publicly traded U.S. companies.

- The Nasdaq-100 Index tracks the 100 largest and most actively traded non-financial domestic and international securities. To be included in the Index, a stock must have a minimum average daily trading volume of 100,000 shares and been listed on stock exchanges for at least two years.

The market can either be up or down. There are some nicknames for the market. A bear market is when the prices are down. A bull market is when the prices are up or expected to go up. A bear market followed the Wall Street Crash of 1929 that led to the Great Depression. People still use the terms bear and bull to describe the markets.

There is a famous "bull" that stands in the financial district in New York City. The "Bowling Green" bull was a gift to the New York Stock Exchange and the city of New York. Two years after the stock market crash of 1987, sculptor Arturo DiModica created the bronze bull and dropped him off in front of the NYSE in the middle of the night. The next morning, the New York Police Department tried to have the bull removed because it was blocking traffic. New Yorkers protested and the city parks department was compelled to grant it "temporary" status at the Bowling Green park, where it remains. Today it serves as an icon of Wall Street, New York City, and the U.S. stock market and is a major tourist attraction.

LINK TO TODAY: Paying for Retirement—Privatized Stocks or Tax-Funded Pensions?

The Social Security Act was proposed by Franklin Delano Roosevelt as part of the New Deal and was passed by Congress in 1935. Its purpose was to guarantee a pension and health insurance that would ensure the elderly against poverty. Today, it also covers those who are disabled and widowed. Funds come from a percentage of employee wages that is matched by employers. The idea behind Social Security is that people pay into the system when they are young and employed so they will have money to live on when they are older and retired. However, due to an aging workforce and recent government budget crises, many fear that the money for the system will not be enough for current and future generations of taxpayers, who will then have nothing for their retirement. Recent proposals would allow young workers to invest the Social Security tax in the stock market instead of putting it into a fund for the older generation. This forces both the young and old into more risky financial futures. Many fear that it will result in future generations of poor, elderly people who do not have enough money to live on. Others believe that it will return financial responsibility to individuals, which is where they believe it belongs. This remains a hotly debated topic in the United States.

Fast Facts

- An American Association of Retired Persons (AARP) survey published in 2011 showed that only 35 percent of adults said they were very or somewhat confident about receiving Social Security benefits in their future.[1]

- In its 2011 *Annual Report,* the Social Security Administration Board of Trustees reported that the program's expenditures had exceeded its non-interest income on 2010 for the first time since 1983 and that trust funds will be exhausted by 2036, after which taxed income will cover about 75 percent of owed benefits through 2085.[2]

- A 2011 study conducted by the Center for Economic and Policy Research in Washington, DC, found that most current pension shortfalls can be traced to the 2007–2009 stock market plunge. The study claims that if those funds had earned the same rate as the interest on a 30-year Treasury bond since 2007, they would be worth $850 billion more than in 2011.[3]

Find and read two newspaper, magazine, or Internet articles, one with positive aspects of Social Security reform and one detailing the negative aspects. Summarize each article. Then write a short paragraph about your personal conclusions.

positive aspects of Social Security reform

_____

_____

_____

_____

negative aspects of Social Security reform

_____

_____

_____

_____

---

[1] Weston, Liz. (2011). Social Security: Fears vs. facts: What Social Security critics keep getting wrong. *AARP: The Magazine,* July/August.

[2] U. S. Social Security Administration (2011). Summary of the 2011 annual reports. www.ssa.gov/oact/trsum/index.html.

[3] Baker, Dean. (February 2011). *The origins and severity of the public pension crisis.* Washington, DC: Center for Economic and Policy Research. www.cepr.net/documents/publications/pensions-2011-02.pdf.

my personal conclusion(s) about Social Security reform in the United States

_____

_____

_____

_____

Putting It All Together

Reflect, and then write your ideas about these questions. Then discuss them in a group.

1. What surprised me most about the Roaring Twenties? About the Great Depression?

_____

_____

2. What does this information help me to understand about modern U.S. American life?

_____

_____

3. Does this information change my opinions about U.S. American values and attitudes? How?

_____

_____

4. Can people in other countries learn something from the lessons the U.S. learned from the Roaring Twenties and the Great Depression? If so, what?

_____

_____

_____

5. What will I tell people if they ask me about the U.S. between World War I and World War II?

_____

_____

_____

6. What positive changes can countries make regarding conservation?

_____

_____

_____

7. What positive policies can countries make to provide for people's retirement needs?

_____

_____

_____

3

The U.S. and World War II

Post-War Consumer Culture, Suburbia, and the Entertainment Industry

Teens learn the latest rock 'n' roll dance moves, 1953. (Photo by Fred Palumbo. Courtesy Library of Congress.)

The U.S. continued to thrive in business and industry, but it also faced a second world war. After the war, life for U.S. American citizens also changed as people moved from cities to suburbs and their entertainment preferences changed.

Net Surfers

To learn more about the time period covered in this unit, search for these names, words, and phrases on the Internet.

all-consuming passion: waking up from the American Dream	post-war baby boom
	the baby boom at mid-decade
Elvis Presley	pop art archive
Graceland	credit card use and debt
Andy Warhol	Sun Studio
Greg Knight's patio culture	FICO
LIFE magazine	credit counseling

Presidential Suite

Franklin Delano Roosevelt (D) 1933–1945
Harry S Truman (D) 1945–1953

On TV

Father Knows Best
Happy Days
Leave It to Beaver

Music Box

"Rock around the Clock"

At the Movies

Grease
Peggy Sue Got Married
Stand by Me

Preparing to Read about Consumer Culture, Suburbia, and the Entertainment Industry

Write some thoughts about these topics, and then discuss them with your classmates.

1. being a consumer

   a. What things do you buy with extra money? _____

   b. What is your favorite commercial or advertisement? Why? _____

   _____

   c. How does your home culture view advertising?

   _____

   d. What is the effect of advertising on your family's spending patterns?

   _____

2. world economies

   a. What product or products have the most influence on the economy in your hometown?_____

   b. How does the economy affect the personal lives of friends and family? _____

   _____

   c. What opportunities are the result of the economy in your family's home country?

   _____

3. population centers

   a. Where do most of the people in your family's home country live? _____

   b. What are the suburbs like? _____

   _____

   c. Does it cost more to live in the cities or in the suburbs there?_____

   _____

   d. Would you prefer to live in a city or in a suburb? Why? _____

   _____

Learning New Vocabulary about the U.S. and World War II

Although this is a long list of words to learn, these words will be helpful to understanding the reading. Review the vocabulary and definitions, and refer to this list as needed.

consumer culture (**n**) lifestyle based on buying and using products

dictator (**n**) leader who takes sole and absolute power, often without being elected

institution (**n**) organization that makes up a society such as a school, government, business, etc.

lack (**n**) not enough of something (most often used as a verb)

suburb (**n**) community outside a city with many houses and schools

to boom (**v**) to grow rapidly

eager (**adj**) very interested in something and wanting to do it quickly

hesitant (**adj**) not sure; not wanting to move quickly

ideological (**adj**) based on ideas or beliefs

immoral (**adj**) not meeting standards of what is good or right in society

scarce (**adj**) little or not enough of

Talking about New Words and Concepts

Take some time to think and talk about new ideas associated with the vocabulary. Then use your understanding of the new vocabulary to discuss each set of questions with a partner.

1. In the United States, the belief in capitalism and democracy is the **ideological** foundation of the government and daily life for most people. Many people will tell you that these beliefs are worth fighting for and that they guarantee freedoms for U.S. American citizens. Others will tell you that they have grown too large and are hurting people who cannot compete against big businesses and the amount of money needed to participate in politics. Ideological foundations that form a basis for people's lives include economic ideologies, political ideologies, religious ideologies, and gender ideologies, to name a few.

   a. What ideological foundation(s) has/have influenced your life the most?

   b. Do most people in your community believe in this/these ideologies?

   c. How do people in your community behave based on these ideologies?

   d. Do you think any ideology in your life (or the lives of those around you) needs to change?

   e. How do you think people in the U.S. behave based on their ideologies?

   f. Do you think the ideology in the U.S. needs to change?

   g. List some words that are related to *ideology*.

2. Anything that does not conform to a society's agreed on moral principles is said to be **immoral** by the majority. These moral principles often have their roots in a country's history. For example, some of the early settlers of the United States were members of a religious group and called themselves Puritans. They had very strict moral codes regarding hard work. This idea is often referred to as the Puritan work ethic. This strict value system still influences many U.S. Americans' public opinions about things such as work, welfare, and independence. Today, many U.S. Americans will tell you that asking for or accepting a handout is against their moral principles because the U.S. is a country that believes in hard work and independence.

   a. What is considered to be immoral by the majority in your community?

   b. Do most people in your community agree with this in their private lives?

   c. Do you think that some things that your grandparents thought were immoral are okay today? What is an example?

d. How do you view U.S. American citizens in terms of morality?

e. Do you think the idea of what is immoral is changing or will change in the U.S.? In your community?

f. List some words that are related to *immoral.*

3. When people move out of the cities into housing communities just outside of the cities, they are said to be moving to the **suburbs**. Many cities in the U.S. have decayed as businesses and people moved away from the city to the suburbs. One example of the result of such movement is a large difference in the quality of schools. Since people who live in the suburbs tend to earn more money than people who live in cities, suburban schools are usually much better than city schools. Part of the reason for this is because money for schools comes from property taxes and property values are higher in the suburbs.

a. Where do most of the people you know live: in cities, suburbs, or rural areas?

b. Do you notice differences in income between people who live in cities, suburbs, and rural areas?

c. What do you think of the tendency of U.S. Americans to move to the suburbs?

d. What are the benefits of such a move for U.S. American citizens? What are some possible drawbacks?

e. List some words that are related to *suburbs.*

4. When something increases rapidly, U.S. Americans say that there is a **boom**. For example, since the 1980s there has been a population boom in the Southwest of the United States. Many people moved from the North to the Southwest because of the warmer weather and businesses moved their offices to take advantage of lower taxes. A boom can also be created by an abundance of a particular product; for example, an oil boom in Texas or a copper boom in Arizona. We might speak of a population boom on a global scale, as the number of people in the world increases rapidly.

a. Has your geographic region ever experienced a boom? What?

b. What was the effect of this boom on your region? Your family? You?

c. List some words that are related to **boom**.

Before Reading: Using a KWL Chart

Using a KWL chart is a good way to organize your thoughts before you read. In the first column, you list things you already know about the topic. In the second column, you list things you want to learn about the topic. The third column is used after you read to collect details that you learned.

Create a KWL chart on a separate piece of paper. List answers to Question 1 in the first column and answers to Question 2 in the second column. Leave the third column empty for now. Then compare answers with your classmates.

1. What do I already know about World War II and the United States?
2. What do I want to know about World War II and the United States?

Reading: The U.S. in World War II and the Consumer Culture

After World War I, the United States began to replace Western Europe as the hub of business and industry. Thus, the 1929 U.S. stock market crash and the economic effects of the Great Depression that followed were felt throughout the world, particularly in Europe. In many countries, such as Russia, Japan, Italy, and Germany, the chaos weakened democratic governments and made room for the rise of **dictators** who promised work, stability, and regained national pride. This was particularly true in Germany, which had suffered a double economic blow due to prior war debts. Adolph Hitler's National Socialist party grew in popularity among the jobless and hungry. Hitler's desire for increased resources and markets led him to invade Poland on September 1, 1939. Within the next three months, Germany invaded Denmark, Norway, Belgium, Luxembourg, The Netherlands, France, Yugoslavia, and Greece. Thus, after a decade of internal focus on lifting itself out of an economic depression, the U.S. was compelled to turn its focus to world events.

The people of the United States were **hesitant** to become involved in another war. Despite divided public opinions, President Roosevelt felt obligated to help the Allies (Great Britain, France, and Russia) in their struggle with the Axis Powers (Italy, Germany, and Japan). In 1941, the United States passed the Lend-Lease Bill that allowed

Famous World War II poster featuring "Rosie the Riveter." Poster by J. Howard Miller. (Courtesy DoD Visual Information Record Center.)

it to sell, lease, and lend more than $50 billion in supplies and weapons to the Allies without officially entering the war. In December of the same year, Japan attacked Pearl Harbor* in Hawaii, which was not yet a U.S. state. The U.S. officially declared war. By September 1945 when the war ended, more than 50 countries had been involved, and it is estimated that more than 55 million people died.

Following the Great Depression, the production needs for fighting with the allied forces in World War II caused industry in the U.S. to **boom**. Factories were producing at full speed, and many women went to work for the first time, learning new skills, earning money, and gaining new confidence. Most U.S. households had **lacked** money during the Great Depression, an era that was followed by **scarce** supplies and food rationing during World War II. Not having anything to spend their factory wages on, many peo-

*Pearl Harbor: a United States naval base

Teenage girls add to graffiti on an Elvis Presley movie poster, 1956. (Photo by Phil Stanziola. Courtesy Library of Congress.)

ple saved; thus, they were able and **eager** to spend money on goods and services that became abundant after the war. An era of large industry, corporate expansion, commercial agriculture, growing universities, and big government arrived. Returning soldiers enrolled in college, bought homes in the new and growing **suburbs**, and financed large appliances to put in their houses, such as refrigerators, washers, and dryers. They purchased automobiles to drive to work in the city. Between 1946–64, they had babies in record numbers, creating a baby-boom generation that fueled the growth of a stable, happy, and prosperous middle class.

In this era of disposable income, what has come to be called the "entertainment industry" began to play a more important role. Some of the products that are often associated with the rise of this industry include Hollywood, films, television, frozen TV dinners, and McDonald's, all of which were successful because middle-class Americans had extra money to spend. The credit card also made its first appearance as a Diner's Club card for restaurant bills. The history of music was changed by a man born into a poor family in Tupelo, Mississippi: Elvis Presley. Up until that time, African Americans in the United States listened to rhythm and blues or jazz music. Bluegrass, country, and big bands were also popular styles in the U.S. Elvis combined these kinds of music for a new sound that became known as rock 'n' roll. Many older people rejected Presley and his music, thinking that it was **immoral**. His dance moves were said to be too explicit, so Elvis was not shown below the waist on television. However, teenagers loved him and his music. Their acceptance of his new style showed early approval of a new kind of social freedom that later exploded in the 1960s, permanently changing values and **institutions** in the United States.

Responding to Information about Consumer Culture, Suburbia, and the Entertainment Industry

When we understand what we read, we often are able to form a picture or an image of what we are reading in our minds. Talking or writing about those images helps us to remember the things we read.

Complete these activities.

1. Use the space to express your reaction to the reading in any way you choose.

2. Take time to complete the third column of the KWL chart. These details may appear later on a test or can help you write about the topic.

Understanding the Reading: Comprehension Check

True/False is a popular way of testing at large, public educational institutions in the United States because instructors can quickly determine who knows the materials and who does not. It is likely that you will encounter this kind of test in U.S. classrooms.

Write T for true or F for false. Discuss why each statement is true or false.

1. The Great Depression in the U.S. ended largely due to World War II in Europe. ____

2. The United States was eager to become involved in World War II. ____

3. World War II involved a handful of European countries and the U.S. ____

4. The only changes in the lives of U.S. citizens after World War II were access to more spending money and living in a country that was a superpower. ____

5. With their extra money, people bought cars, homes, and appliances. ____

6. The middle class in the United States became smaller after World War II. ____

7. The entertainment industry fueled Hollywood, McDonald's, and TV dinners. ____

8. Everybody loved Elvis Presley's new kind of music. ____

9. Rock 'n' roll contributed to public value changes in the U.S. after World War II. ____

Looking at Consumer Culture: Andy Warhol's Pop Art

Andy Warhola, Jr., the son of Czech immigrants, was born in 1928 in Pittsburgh, Pennsylvania. His father died when Andy was 14, so he worked his way through art school at the Carnegie Institute of Technology on a scholarship and had a job at a dairy store creating window displays. Wanting to be famous, he Americanized his name after moving to New York City. He did commercial art and window displays for a few years until pop art spread from Britain to New York in the late 1950s. By the 1960s, a distinctly U.S. style of pop art had emerged.

The post-war boom in the American economy and the extra purchasing power of the people brought aggressive media advertising. Companies began to mass-market products to a mass consumer audience. Andy Warhol and other pop artists, such as Roy Lichtenstein, Jasper Johns, James Rosenquist, and Robert Rauschenberg, responded to these trends by producing bold, repetitive, mechanical art that included prints, cartoons, and lithography. It was intended to parody and satirize the audience by impersonalizing popular people and turning them into objects. Their response to the post-war consumer trend grew into a famous commentary on the buying habits of U.S. American citizens. Ironically, in 2009, a private collector bought one of Warhol's paintings called *Eight Elvises* for $100 million.

An example of pop art by Lichtenstein.

Talking about Art

The Andy Warhol Museum in Pittsburgh, Pennsylvania, is affiliated with the Carnegie Institute. It is the largest museum in the United States dedicated to the work of one artist. It contains 17 galleries with 900 paintings, 1,000 prints, 77 sculptures, and 4,000 photographs by Warhol.

Visit the Andy Warhol Museum at www.warhol.org to see some of his famous, colorful paintings. Be sure to look for his portrayals of Marilyn Monroe, Elvis Presley, Jackie Kennedy, Campbell's soup cans, Coke bottles, Brillo soap pad boxes, shoes, and dollar bills. (Licensing and copyright laws prevent us from reprinting any art by Andy Warhol.) Choose one painting by Andy Warhol. Then answer the questions.

1. What is Warhol's main message to the audience?

   _____

   _____

2. What specific aspect of society is being criticized?

   _____

   _____

3. Is the criticism harsh and direct or soft and indirect?

   _____

   _____

LANGUAGE FOCUS: Using Hedging Techniques to Express Your Own Critical Observations

Native speakers of U.S. American English are generally a little less direct about expressing critical observations than native speakers of other languages. Often, they are surprised and sometimes offended at what they think is inappropriate directness of non-native speakers. While it is acceptable in U.S. American society to make positive and negative observations—and is even insisted upon in U.S. American classroom settings when discussing ideas and class readings—it is accomplished appropriately by a technique called *hedging*. Hedging makes observations less direct by softening the statements with a positive observation that balances out the negative. Some good hedging words to begin with are:

> *Although . . .*
>
> *Even though . . .*
>
> *Though . . .*
>
> *While . . .*

The effect these words have on critical observations is evident when comparing these two sentences about Andy Warhol paintings:

> Positive Observation: *The subject is interesting.*
>
> Critical Observation: *The colors in the painting are annoying.*
>
> Hedged Critical Observation: *Although the subject is interesting, the colors in the painting are annoying.*

Other hedging words can be used as well.

> **Even though** *the subject is interesting, the colors in the painting are annoying.*
>
> **Though** *the subject is interesting, the colors in the painting are annoying.*
>
> **While** *the subject is interesting, the colors in the painting are annoying.*

1. Make a list of five positive and five negative observations about the piece of Andy Warhol work you chose.

Positive Observations Example: *The subject is interesting.*	Negative Observations Example: *The colors are annoying.*
1.	1.
2.	2.
3.	3.
4.	4.
5.	5.

2. Now place one of the hedging words or phrases before any one of the positive observations, add a comma, and then state one of the negative observations.

   Example: ***Although*** *the subject is interesting, the colors are annoying.*

   1.
   2.
   3.
   4.
   5.

3. How can learning to express criticism more politely change the effect you have on the listener when speaking English? List some situations in which you think using hedging techniques can be a good idea.

   _____

   _____

   _____

4. Based on what you have learned about softening criticism and based on your answer to the question about Andy Warhol's kind of criticism, what kind of effect do you think his art had on the viewing public?

   _____

   _____

   _____

LINK TO TODAY: Credit Card Nation in Crisis—How Much Is Too Much?

Since World War II, consuming seems to be almost a matter of obligation in U.S. American society and cash has largely fallen out of fashion. It is nearly impossible to live and conduct business in the U.S without a credit card. Some popular credit cards in the United States are Visa, MasterCard, American Express, and Discover. In the United States, it is important to build a good credit history, which is measured by your **credit score**. This score can determine the interest rate on a bank loan or affect being hired for a job. Each person has three credit scores—Equifax, Experion, and Transunion—that are tied to a Social Security number. If you have a loan or credit card, it is a good idea to check your credit scores every year to make sure there is no false information and that you have not been a victim of identity theft. Generally speaking, a good credit score is 700 or above.

Until the 2007–2009 economic crisis, it was very easy to obtain a credit card. It was not uncommon to get multiple card offers in the mail or to be offered a gift such as a free product or t-shirt for filling out credit card applications on college campuses, at shopping malls, or in airports. This information was often sold to other marketing companies, who then advertised their products and services in the mail or over the phone (telemarketing). The recent economic downturn has resulted in a "credit crunch" that has made obtaining credit more difficult—especially for people with low credit scores or no credit history. The crisis has also made thrifty spending and cash payment fashionable again. One thing about life in the United States that does not change over time is that advertisers want money from consumers. It is a good idea to be careful about giving out personal information or buying things via mail, telephone, or the Internet, especially if you do not understand completely what is being offered. Many people, including native speakers, have been victims of illegal marketing scams.

Fast Facts

- The U.S. Congress passed the Credit Card Act in May 2009, with support from both major political parties in both the House of Representatives and the Senate. The law protects consumers against unfair or deceptive credit practices and restricts penalties, late charges, and interest rate hikes.

- The U.S. Federal Trade Commission gave a $1.13 million grant to the University of Missouri to conduct research into the fairness and efficiency with which credit score disputes are handled in support of the Fair Credit Reporting Act.[2]

---

[1] http://101-credit-cards.com/credit-cards-articles/a-new-academic-study-scrutinizes-credit-score-reporting.

[2] Consumer Financial Protection Bureau. (February 2011). CARD Act Factsheet. www.consumerfinanace.gov/credit-cards/credit-card-act/feb2011-factsheet/.

- A 2011 study by Pew Charitable Trusts found that credit card late payment fees decreased and interest rates stabilized as a result of the 2009 Credit CARD Act legislation.[3]
- A U.S. Commerce Department report showed that consumer spending was down at the start of 2012 as compared to previous years.[4]
- The U.S. Federal Reserve estimated in 2011 that consumer debt was more than $2.4 trillion at the end of 2011, with the average household having $6,500 in credit card debt in 2010.[5]

Find and read two newspaper, magazine, or Internet articles, one with positive aspects of credit cards and one detailing the negative aspects. Summarize each article. Then write a short paragraph about your personal conclusions.

positive aspects of credit cards

_____

_____

_____

_____

negative aspects of credit cards

_____

_____

_____

_____

my personal conclusion(s) about credit cards in the United States

_____

_____

_____

_____

[2] Pew Charitable Trust Safe Credit Cards Project (2011). Washington, DC. www.pewtrusts.org/news_room_detail.aspx?id=85899359571.

[3] U.S. Department of Commerce Bureau of Economic Analysis. (2012). *Personal income and outlays, December 2011.* www.bea.gov/newsreleases/national/pi/pinewsrelease.htm.

[4] U.S. Federal Reserve Board of Governors. (2011). *G-19 Release Consumer Credit.* http://www.federalreserve.gov/releases/g19/Current/.

Putting It All Together

Reflect, and then write your ideas about these questions. Then discuss them in a group.

1. What surprised me most about the information regarding post-war consumer culture in the United States?

   _____

   _____

2. What does this information help me to understand about modern U.S. American life?

   _____

   _____

3. Does this information change my opinions about U.S. American values and attitudes? How?

   _____

   _____

4. Can people in other countries learn something from the effects of U.S. American consumer culture?

   _____

   _____

5. What will I tell people if they ask me about consumerism in the United States?

   _____

   _____

6. What positive changes can countries make regarding consumerism? Should they make any changes at all?

   _____

   _____

4

The U.S. at Midcentury

Desegregation and the Demand for Equality and Civil Rights

Dr. Martin Luther King, Jr., speaks out for civil rights. (Photo by Dick DeMarsico. Courtesy Library of Congress.)

Although the U.S. claimed victory fighting overseas in World War II, many problems at home remained unsolved. There is some overlap in content in Units 3 and 4. This unit is about social problems affecting this era that dated back to the previous century and the hope of making positive changes.

Net Surfers

To learn more about the time period covered in this unit, search for these names, words, and phrases on the Internet.

affirmative action
affirmative action and college
    admissions
the U.S. Civil War
the Emancipation Proclamation
Jim Crow America
Jim Crow laws

Ku Klux Klan
Martin Luther King, Jr.
the Montgomery bus boycott
1957 desegregation in Little Rock,
    Arkansas
Rosa Parks

★ ──────────────────────────── ★

Presidential Suite

Dwight D. Eisenhower (R) 1953–1961
John F. Kennedy (D) 1961–1963
(Refer also to Abraham Lincoln (R) 1861–1865)

★ ──────────────────────────── ★

On TV

I'll Fly Away

★ ──────────────────────────── ★

Music Box

"We Shall Overcome"

★ ──────────────────────────── ★

At the Movies

The Long Walk Home
Malcolm X
Mississippi Burning
To Kill a Mockingbird (adapted from a novel)

★ ──────────────────────────── ★

Preparing to Read about Desegregation and the Demand for Equality and Civil Rights

Write some thoughts about these topics, and then discuss them with your classmates.

1. racism and society

   a. What is the racial make-up of the population in your family's home country?

   _____

   b. Is there a history of laws related to race in that country?

   _____

   c. What negative effects of racism have been noted in that country?

   _____

   d. Has your family's country had any positive experiences with race relations?

   _____

2. social change, progress, and resistance

   a. What kind of widescale social changes have been noted in your family's home country? _____

   _____

   b. What changes would you like to see regarding race relations in your community?

   _____

3. human and civil rights

   a. What rights do you think are necessary for every person? _____

   _____

   b. What rights do you believe are being denied to people in the world? _____

   _____

   c. What rights are you willing to fight for? _____

   _____

   d. Is there anything that you think should not be a universal human right? Should certain rights be denied to anybody for any reason? _____

   _____

Learning New Vocabulary about the U.S. at Midcentury

Although this is a long list of words to learn, these words will be helpful to understanding the reading. Preview the vocabulary and definitions, and refer to this list as needed.

boycott (n) organized refusal to use a product or service

clash (n) confrontational disagreement

discrimination (n) exclusion based on race, gender, religion, etc.

emancipation (n) the act of setting somebody or something free

inequality (n) state of not being equal or the same

segregation (n) the act of separating people or things from one another

to assassinate (v) to murder

to enforce (v) to back up or support

to exercise (v) to put into action

to forbid (v) to not allow

to integrate (v) to put together

to linger (v) to stay around; to not go away

to pen (v) to write

to prevent (v) to keep somebody from doing something

to segregate (v) to prevent different people from interacting

to stand up for (v) to support; to demand

to violate (v) to break the law

complicated (adj) not easy; difficult to figure out

constitutional (adj) allowed by the U.S. Constitution; fits the ideas of the Constitution

entrenched (adj) deep

federal (adj) controlled on a country-wide basis instead of by individual communities, cities, or states

touchstone (adj) central

unconstitutional (adj) not allowed by the U.S. Constitution; against the ideas of the Constitution

Talking about New Words and Concepts

Take some time to think and talk about new ideas associated with the vocabulary. Then use your understanding of the new vocabulary to discuss each set of questions with a partner.

1. In the United States, boycotting has been an effective tool for causing social change. It usually works because it is based on economic factors. One national **boycott** was led by César Chávez. He wanted to achieve better working conditions for grape pickers and other agricultural workers in California, who were mostly Hispanic. Local boycotts of businesses or products are often helpful in changing unfair practices as well, since a business needs local support to survive.

   a. Are boycotts viewed as effective tools for change in your community?

   b. Can you think of examples when people used boycotts to change things? List them.

   c. What was the reason for the boycott?

   d. Were the goals of the boycott achieved?

   e. Would you participate in a boycott? Why or why not?

   f. List some words that are related to *boycott.*

2. **Discrimination** is illegal in the United States, and there are many public statements at businesses and schools made against it. These statements often read something like: "We do not discriminate on the basis of race, nationality, ethnicity, age, gender, religion, disabilities, marital status, veteran status, sexual orientation, etc."

   a. Are any of these kinds of discrimination practiced in your community, regardless of laws?

   b. Do you think that any of these kinds of discrimination are still practiced in the U.S.?

   c. Have you experienced discrimination personally?

   d. Do you think that more change is needed in eliminating discrimination?

   e. What can people do to help stop discrimination?

   f. List some words that are related to *discrimination.*

3. If you support something or demand it, you **stand up for** it. You may notice that parents in the U.S. often encourage their children to stand up for themselves and their rights. This is considered to be a necessary skill and part of becoming an involved adult in U.S. society. It is generally not considered rude or problematic as long as the person does not break laws or harm others.

   a. Are people encouraged or discouraged to stand up for themselves in your community?

   b. What is the social result of demanding individual rights?

   c. Do you think that standing up for individual rights has a positive or negative effect on society in general?

   d. What rights of your own have you stood up for? What was the result?

   e. List some words that are related to *standing up for*.

4. When things are kept apart because of laws or societal expectations, they are segregated. In the United States, **segregation** based on race is no longer legal. However, there is still some gender segregation enforced by law (such as public restrooms). Other kinds of segregation exist because of social and/or economic factors, even though there are no specific laws about it. For example, people who live in suburbs are socially segregated from people who live in inner cities, even though laws don't prevent them from interacting.

   a. What kinds of segregation (legal or social) exist in your community?

   b. Do people ever complain about this segregation?

   c. What have they tried to do about it? Were they successful?

   d. Do you see evidence of racial segregation in the United States, even though it is illegal?

   e. List some words that are related to *segregation*.

5. When people in the same situation don't receive the same benefits or treatment there is **inequality.** Despite laws that try to eliminate inequality in the United States, many people still believe that inequality exists for social or cultural reasons. For example, many females and minorities in U.S. schools do not take advanced math and science classes even though they are allowed and encouraged to. Today, school counselors and teachers try to deal with the cultural and social reasons for this inequality by breaking stereotypes about who should take these courses.

   a. Are there examples of social or cultural inequality in your community?

   b. Are people satisfied with this kind of inequality? If not, what have they tried to do about it?

   c. Do you think that some kinds of inequality (like gender) are determined more by society or by biology/nature?

   d. Is it possible for people to eliminate inequality?

   e. List some words that are related to *inequality*.

Before Reading: Mind Mapping

A mind map is a diagram of some sort that helps give a visual representation of ideas. Usually one key word is in the middle and related events, ideas, or questions extend from it. Using a mind map helps you focus on the reading and make predictions.

Make a mind map for discrimination. Write events, ideas, or questions that are related to discrimination. Note places where they may overlap with each other. Based on this mind map, make a list of ideas that you expect the reading to address.

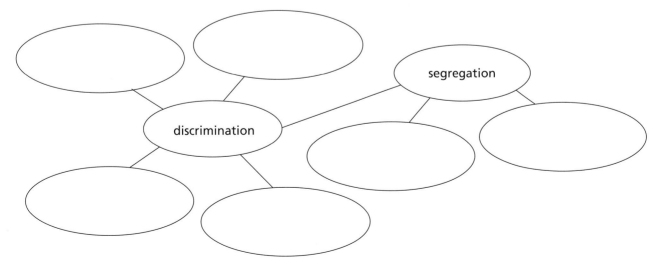

Reading: The United States at Midcentury

Even though there was a consumer boom and a rapidly growing middle class in the United States after World War II, long **lingering** ideas about racial differences **prevented** many from enjoying America's new found prosperity. Despite large-scale social progress, many parts of the country still contained pockets of poverty and glaring racial **discrimination**. Deep racial divisions had existed since the founding of the nation, largely due to the institution of slavery. These ideological divisions came to a head in 1861, when several Southern states attempted to form their own country—the Confederate States of America—so they could make their own laws regarding the ownership of slaves. During the war, President Abraham Lincoln **penned** the 1863 **Emancipation Proclamation** that legally freed and gave citizenship to former slaves in the northern states. This was **reinforced** by the Thirteenth Amendment to the Constitution (making African Americans full citizens), the Fourteenth (guaranteeing equal protection under the law), and the Fifteenth (**forbidding** racial discrimination in access to voting). The four-year War Between the States (now referred to as the Civil War) was eventually won by the North, and the emancipation laws extended to the South as well. This era left scars that were still very evident by the mid-twentieth century.

In 1950, two-thirds of the African-American population lived in the South. Even

A clear Civil War division line between North and South near Chattanooga, Tennessee, 1864. (Courtesy DoD Visual Information Record Center.)

though slavery no longer legally existed, many black citizens still faced **entrenched** social and political discrimination. All U.S. states must follow federal law, but if there are no laws on an issue, each state also has the right to make its own. This is how the Ku Klux Klan and "Jim Crow laws" became stronger in some Southern states. These laws were made by local leaders in indi-

President Abraham Lincoln signed the Emancipation Proclamation in 1863. (Photo by Matthew Brady. Courtesy DoD Visual Information Record Center.)

vidual states to keep blacks and whites away from each other in public areas without **violating federal** laws. Jim Crow laws legally forced blacks and whites to use separate public restrooms, separate drinking fountains, and separate waiting rooms. Trains, buses, and restaurants had "whites only" and "colored only" sections. Black children were not allowed to go to school with white children. **Complicated** rules stated that people could vote only if their grandparents had voted. This unfairly affected blacks because their grandparents had not legally been citizens and therefore not eligible to vote. In addition, threats to blacks by whites prevented many African-American citizens from **exercising** their legal voting rights.

The public separation caused by Jim Crow laws was questioned in many courts. The U.S. Supreme Court had ruled as early as 1892 that "separate but equal" was **constitutional**. This meant that it was legal in the U.S. for different facilities to exist for blacks and whites, as long as they were of similar quality. Due partly to increased social consciousness and public protest, the Supreme Court eventually reversed its decision and ruled that "separate but equal" was **unconstitutional** in 1954. This paved the way for challenges to school **segregation**. In the 1954 case of *Brown* v. *Board of Education* in Topeka, Kansas, the Supreme Court ruled that school segregation was unconstitutional. Despite a growing number of federal laws, local practices remained discriminatory in almost every aspect of public life. Rosa Parks (an African-American U.S. citizen) boarded a bus in Montgomery, Alabama, and sat in the "whites only" section one day

Protests like this became common in the 1960s in the fight for civil rights. (Courtesy Library of Congress.)

after work in 1955. When a white man ordered her to move to the back of the bus, she refused and was arrested by the police. Because of her arrest and the discrimination of the bus company, civil rights activists organized a year-long **boycott** of the buses, causing the bus company to lose a lot of money. But even this was not enough to change things. Eventually, the Supreme Court specifically declared that segregation of transportation was unconstitutional.

In 1957, the first attempt to **integrate** schools was at Little Rock High School in Little Rock, Arkansas. There, people protested school integration violently, and the governor called in Arkansas National Guard soldiers to block the door to the school in order to prevent nine black students from entering the all-white school. President Eisenhower **enforced** the federal law by sending U.S. army soldiers to protect the students and escort them to class. Despite this victory, efforts to integrate schools were slow. Some universities in the Deep South remained all-white as late as 1963, when Governor George C. Wallace of Alabama stood in the doorway of the University of Alabama shouting, "Segregation now! Segregation tomorrow! Segregation forever!" to prevent two African-American students from taking classes at the university.

African-American leaders such as Dr. Martin Luther King, Jr., encouraged his followers to **stand up for** equal rights through peaceful protest. During the late 1950s and 1960s, scores of individuals organized marches on Washington, DC, sit-ins* at segregated lunch counters, and campaigns to register voters. Freedom Riders boarded on busses with the goal of integrating them. Each instance resulted in injury and sometimes death due to violent **clashes** with police and opposition groups. A 1963 bombing of the 16th Street Baptist Church in Birmingham, Alabama, killed four innocent schoolgirls. Over the course of the decade, several organized voting registration marches from Selma to Montgomery ended violently. The movement lost its **touchstone** leader in 1968, when Martin Luther King, Jr., was **assassinated** at his Memphis hotel. During the course of the movement, several Civil Rights Acts were signed into law by Presidents Kennedy and Johnson. Although many people today believe that U.S. schools and American society are desegregated, others argue that inequality still exists in U.S. institutions.

---

*sit-ins: protest in which participants occupy an establishment and often involves sitting on the floor

---

Responding to Information about Desegregation and the Demand for Equality and Civil Rights

One way to use information from reading is to make connections from the reading to life.

Complete these activities.

1. What does the information in the text remind you of in your personal life? Write a paragraph about it on a separate sheet of paper.

Understanding the Reading: Comprehension Check

If you have taken or studied for the TOEFL® exam, you are familiar with multiple choice testing. Questions on a multiple choice test each contain a "stem" and several answer choices. The correct choice is the answer, and the others are called "distractors." Usually, one distractor is obviously wrong while the other two are more or less possible. The goal of the multiple choice test is to choose the best answer.

Use your understanding of the reading to eliminate the distractors, and a circle the one best answer for each question.

1. What is a Jim Crow law?

   a. a law against shooting birds

   b. a law forcing racial separation in public

   c. a law making slavery illegal

   d. a law separating children at school

2. African-American children living in the southern U.S. in the early 1950s were *not* allowed to _____.

   a. go to school

   b. go to school with other black children

   c. go to school with white children

   d. go to school on a bus

3. What does the phrase *separate but equal* mean?

   a. Different public places for black and white citizens were constitutional if the quality was similar.

   b. Different public places for black and white citizens were not constitutional.

   c. Different public places for black and white citizens were not equal.

   d. Different public places for black and white citizens did not exist.

4. The result of the Montgomery bus boycott was _____.

   a. the Supreme Court voted against segregation

   b. the bus company lost a lot of money when African Americans stopped riding the buses

   c. the bus company was concerned about the comfort of customers

   d. a lot of bad publicity for the bus company from Rosa Parks' arrest

5. What did desegregation laws in U.S. American schools result in?

   a. protests by whites

   b. protests by blacks

   c. protests by the government

   d. protests by the teachers

6. Where was the first school in the United States to be desegregated located?

   a. Montgomery, Alabama

   b. Topeka, Kansas

   c. Little Rock, Arkansas

   d. Hooper, Utah

7. The governor of Arkansas tried to prevent nine black children from attending school by _____.

   a. holding the front door open to them

   b. telling them to go home

   c. standing in the doorway shouting, "Segregation forever!"

   d. bringing in Arkansas National Guard soldiers to block the doorway

8. In order to make sure that black children were allowed into white schools, President Eisenhower _____.

   a. sent federal troops to accompany the students to class

   b. had a friendly chat with the Arkansas governor

   c. signed a new federal bill requiring schools to register black children

   d. did nothing and hoped for the best

9. When did the University of Alabama begin to allow black students to study there?

   a. 1863

   b. 1950

   c. 1955

   d. 1963

10. What is the phrase that best describes racial attitudes in the United States after World War II?

    a. open and tolerant

    b. bitter and helpless

    c. confused but progressive

    d. joyful but painful

Learning More about Martin Luther King, Jr.'s "I Have a Dream" Speech

Martin Luther King, Jr., gave a famous speech at the Lincoln Memorial in Washington, DC, on August 28, 1963. His famous "I Have a Dream" speech is available from many sites online. (Due to copyright issues, we are unable to print even a portion of the speech in this book.)

Talking about King's Dream

Find a copy of the speech, and read the paragraph starting with the words "I have a dream that one day this nation will rise up . . . ", which is considered the most famous part of this speech.

Read or listen to the speech online and answer these questions.

1. What is King's main message to the people?

   _____

   _____

2. Do you think that his dream came true in the United States? Give one example of how his dream came true. Give one example of how it has not.

   _____

   _____

3. If you are able to find a video of King giving the speech, what do you notice about the way King delivers the speech? What kind of body language and voice does he use? What effect does it have on the listener?

   _____

   _____

LANGUAGE FOCUS: Using Parallelism

The "I Have a Dream" speech is powerful and moving. Some people associate the word *dream* with the ideas of this speech. One linguistic/rhetorical factor that makes King's speech very focused on the dream is that he repeated the same introductory phrase *I have a dream that . . .* several times. This is a technique called *parallelism,* and it is used by speakers and writers of English to focus the listener's or reader's attention.

Many people have dreams. Some may want to be famous or rich. Others may be more concerned with global issues and dream of a world with no war or hunger. Dreams are an important part of life.

1. What is your dream? Write a speech about your own dreams, using parallelism when possible to keep the listener focused on your dream.

   I have a dream that one day . . .

   I have a dream that people will be able to . . .

   I have a dream today . . .

2. Deliver your speech to your classmates.

Conducting a Survey

Surveys are a good way to get information about people's attitudes toward various ideas. You will notice that surveys are common in the United States. Newspapers and websites often report results of polling information, consumer groups often survey customers at local shopping centers, and organizations sometimes call and conduct telephone surveys on various topics. Many Americans are happy to answer survey questions if they have time and if the surveyor is polite and gives them some information about the purpose of the survey. Most, however, do not like to be surveyed over the phone. U.S. students tend to be very willing to help out if they know that the information is used for a class project. Keep in mind, though, that race issues can be very sensitive in any population.

Look at this sample survey. Decide what questions you have about civil rights. Conduct your own survey by asking three classmates to answer the questions.

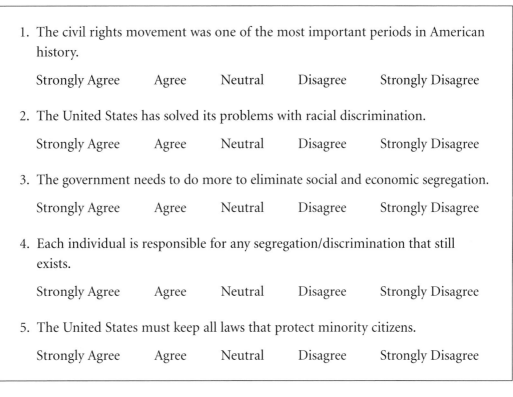

1. The civil rights movement was one of the most important periods in American history.

   Strongly Agree   Agree   Neutral   Disagree   Strongly Disagree

2. The United States has solved its problems with racial discrimination.

   Strongly Agree   Agree   Neutral   Disagree   Strongly Disagree

3. The government needs to do more to eliminate social and economic segregation.

   Strongly Agree   Agree   Neutral   Disagree   Strongly Disagree

4. Each individual is responsible for any segregation/discrimination that still exists.

   Strongly Agree   Agree   Neutral   Disagree   Strongly Disagree

5. The United States must keep all laws that protect minority citizens.

   Strongly Agree   Agree   Neutral   Disagree   Strongly Disagree

Bring your survey and results to class. Share them with a small group. Talk about the similarities and differences. Summarize your group's results for the class.

LINK TO TODAY: Affirmative Action and American Public Life— Who Should Benefit?

Affirmative action laws were one result of the civil rights movement. They were designed to help create racial and gender balance in public life by helping minorities and women gain access to America's top schools, jobs, and public programs. Federal affirmative action laws state that employers must take steps to recruit and advance qualified minorities, women, persons with disabilities, and veterans. Affirmative actions include training programs and outreach efforts. Affirmative action in all aspects of public life has become very controversial. Many people argue that this is "reverse discrimination," which makes it difficult for qualified white males to get positions. Others are concerned that such programs make the success of women and minorities seem unearned.

In 1996, California citizens voted yes on Proposition 209. This state law was designed to eliminate affirmative action, making it illegal to give racial preference in California university admissions; now, admissions are based only on grades and test scores. Opponents of the new laws have argued that the tests are racially biased and that all of the progress made by women and minorities since the civil rights movement will disappear if they are used as the only factor in college admissions and job hiring. Other states are considering similar laws, and many challenges are being made in state and federal courts. The U.S. Supreme Court may need to determine a national policy.

Fast Facts

- Several states, including California, Washington, Michigan, Nebraska, and Arizona (as of 2012) have or had anti-affirmative action laws that ensure that admission decisions to schools, jobs, and other public programs based solely on merit and not race or gender.

- A 2009 Carnegie Mellon study indicated that a ban on affirmative action would have little effect on enrollments for traditional students but would decrease the number of minorities at top-tier universities by more than 30 percent.[1]

- A 2011 U.S. Supreme Court ruling gave public and private universities the right to use race as a factor in student admissions for another 25 years.[2]

---

[1] Burd, Mark. (2009). *Universal ban on affirmative action would shrink minority presence at top-tier colleges by more than one-third.* Pittsburgh: Tepper School of Business, Carnegie Mellon University. http://www.cmu.edu/news/archive/2009/January/jan14_affirmativeactionstudy.shtml.

[2] *Federal Observer.* (2011). Affirmative Action: The U.S. still struggles to bridge the achievement gap in higher education. www.federalobserver.com/2011/01/17/affirmative-action-the-u-s-still-struggles-to-bridge-the-achievement-gap-in-higher-education/.

- Texas has a Top Ten Percent plan. The Top Ten Percent plan means that graduates in the top ten percent of their graduating class in high school are granted admittance to the public university or college of their choice. Statistics from the 2008 admissions cycle at University of Texas show that of the 363 African-American freshmen from Texas admitted and enrolled, 305 were the product of the Top Ten Percent plan, and just 58 were admitted through merit or a combination of merit and race. For in-state Hispanics, 1,322 were admitted through the Top Ten Percent plan and just 158 through merit or a combination of merit and ethnicity.[3]

Find and read two newspaper, magazine, or Internet articles, one with positive aspects of affirmative action and one detailing the negative aspects. Summarize each article. Then write a short paragraph about your personal conclusions.

positive aspects of affirmative action

_____

_____

_____

_____

negative aspects of affirmative action

_____

_____

_____

_____

my personal conclusions about affirmative action in the United States

_____

_____

_____

_____

_____

[3] Kahlenberg, Richard. (2011). "The next big affirmative-action case." _Chronicle of Higher Education._ http://chronicle.com/blogs/innovations/the-next-big-affirmative-action-case/28476.

Putting It All Together

Reflect, and then write your ideas about these questions. Then discuss them in a group.

1. What surprised me most about the U.S. civil rights movement?

   _____

   _____

2. What does this information help me to understand about modern U.S. American life?

   _____

   _____

3. Does this information change my opinions about U.S. American values and attitudes? How?

   _____

   _____

4. Can people in other countries learn something from the lessons U.S. Americans learned from the civil rights movement?

   _____

   _____

5. What will I tell people if they ask me about race issues in the United States?

   _____

   _____

6. What positive changes can countries make regarding racial discrimination? Should they make any changes at all?

   _____

   _____

5 The U.S. Counterrevolution of the Sixties

The Generation of Flower Power, Universal Love, and Woodstock

Poster for Woodstock Festival, July, 1969. (Courtesy Library of Congress.)

The sixties are known as the era of the counterrevolution in the U.S. and is one of the most romanticized eras of U.S. history despite the generational conflict that was part of it.

Net Surfers

To learn more about the time period covered in this unit, search for these names, words, and phrases on the Internet.

beat generation writers	postcards from Route 66
1960s hippies	Sixties slang
Jack Kerouac	Woodstock
Jack Kerouac's Windblown World	Sixties music
Martin's Route 66 gallery and essay	Sixties counterculture
National Historic Route 66 Federation	flower children
U.S. Route 66	urban problems of the 1960s

Presidential Suite

John F. Kennedy (D) 1961–1963
Lyndon B. Johnson (D) 1963–1969
Richard M. Nixon (R) 1969–1974

On TV

The Wonder Years

Music Box

"Aquarius"—The Fifth Dimension
"Blowin' in the Wind"—Bob Dylan
"Route 66"—Bobby Troupe
"San Francisco"—Scott McKenzie
"The Times They Are A-Changin'"—Bob Dylan
"Turn, Turn, Turn"—The Byrds
"Volunteers"—Jefferson Airplane

Preparing to Read about the Generation of Flower Power, Universal Love, and Woodstock

Write some thoughts about these topics, and then discuss them with your classmates.

1. social rebels in society

   a. What kind of people are considered to be outside of the "norm" in your family's home country?

   _____

   _____

   b. How do they look, dress, act, and think?

   _____

   _____

2. authority and social institutions

   a. Who occupies a place of authority in your life?

   _____

   b. How do you interact with and react to the presence of this authority?

   _____

   c. Have you ever chosen to disobey authority? If so, were there serious consequences?

   _____

   _____

   d. Who do you think should have a place of authority in your life? Is there anyone that should not?

   _____

   _____

3. self-expression

   a. When do you think that self-expression becomes offensive to others? When that happens, what should be done? _____

   _____

   b. How do you like to express yourself? _____

   _____

Learning New Vocabulary about the U.S. Counterrevolution of the Sixties

Although this is a long list of words to learn, these words will be helpful to understanding the reading. Preview the vocabulary and definitions, and refer to the list as needed.

activism (n) belief in making social changes according to one's ideas

commune (n) shared living situation involving unrelated people; everyone gives what they have and takes what they need

consumerism (n) attitude that values using instead of saving or preserving

counterrevolution (n) movement to make U.S. American society more liberal and open; also called the Hippie Movement

deception (n) a lie or cover up

disillusionment (n) loss of belief in one's faith, country, governement, parents, or society

establishment (n) something that is a foundation of society; schools and institutions are good examples

flower children (n) name given to the less political, more romantic hippies

hierarchy (n) the social order with authority on top and regular people on bottom

hippie (n) representative of the counterrevolution—a liberal member of society, especially that in the 1960s

interconnectedness (n) a state of being connected or attached to and through other things

mantra (n) a word or group of words regarded as capable of creating transformation

materialism (n) attitude that values money and purchased items

non-conformity (n) not doing the same thing as the mainstream

restlessness (n) need to go to different places and try different things; inability to settle into a routine

sexism (n) belief that men are better than women (or vice versa)

teach-in (n) a gathering of protesters who sit in large groups and educate the public about their ideas and goals

tension (n) conflict or pressure

to detach (v) to separate from

to drop out (v) to stop attending school; to stop participating in society (*dropout* is the noun)

to hitchhike (v) to travel by asking for a ride from other people, most often strangers

to politicize (v) to make something that has not traditionally been political a focus of politics or political issues

romanticized (adj) having a dreamy and idealistic appearance or idea even if it is actually more serious

unprecedented (adj) not seen or not occurring before

Talking about New Words and Concepts

Take some time to think and talk about new ideas associated with the vocabulary. Then use your understanding of the new vocabulary to discuss each set of questions with a partner.

1. Since World War II, the United States has been the world leader in **consumerism,** using the most raw materials and natural resources in the world. In recent years, other countries, especially in Asia, have begun to catch up with and even surpass the U.S. in the use of raw materials. A growing number of people are beginning to worry about the social and environmental effects of this trend.

   a. What effects of consumerism do you see in U.S. society?

   b. Do you think that these effects will create problems in the future?

   c. How do people in your community view U.S. consumerism?

   d. Do you think that your family's country of origin is becoming more consumer oriented? How about your relatives and friends?

   e. If this is a problem in your community, what can you and those around you do to stop or slow it?

   f. List some words that are related to *consumerism.*

2. **Sexism** refers to the belief that one gender is better than another and practices that come from or support that idea. Sexist attitudes especially bother the majority of American women, who expect to be treated with respect and equality both in public and at home.

   a. Can you think of examples of sexism in the United States?

   b. Does sexism exist in your community? What evidence do you see that it does or does not?

   c. How can people make changes that allow more equality between men and women? Should they make such changes? Why or why not?

   d. List some words that are related to *sexism.*

3. The word **establishment** refers to the individual institutions that make a community, such as businesses, schools, and churches. In the 1960s, the hippies used this word to describe the traditional codes of a white, male-dominated U.S. society. Most of the rebellion of this time period was directed against **"the establishment."** The adjective *established* is used today to refer to ideas that are common to the culture of the U.S. and generally understood by its citizens.

   a. What does the establishment in your community think?

   b. Do you believe that the establishment in your community is too rigid or too flexible? If so, how?

   c. List some words that are related to *establishment.*

4. In the 1960s, a common form of protest was called a **teach-in.** This was a peaceful activity, mostly on university campuses, where students sat together and talked about their viewpoints on various issues instead of going to class. Often, student activists would teach the others about the issues concerning them and ask other students for support in protesting them.

   a. Do you think that this kind of activism can be effective?

   b. Are young people or students in your community allowed to organize or to participate in such activities? Why or why not? What usually happens if people protest?

   c. Would you be interested in going to a teach-in?

   d. List some words that are related to *teach-in.*

5. When people lose faith in any aspect of their government, family, or selves, they are experiencing **disillusionment.** The hippies had little faith in the ability of the older generations or of the government to make the right legal, moral, and social decisions for them to follow. They rejected the old values and searched for better ways of doing things. This is common in every generation, but it was never as public, nor as organized as it was in 1960s America.

   a. Do you think that U.S. Americans are disillusioned today? What evidence do you see of this?

   b. Are you disillusioned with any aspect of your life?

   c. Are the young people in your community disillusioned with your government? If so, what evidence do you see of this?

   d. Can people reject the old ways and make a change? Should they?

   e. List some words that are related to *disillusionment.*

6. Even today, a person who is idealistic and does not conform to the **materialistic** consumerism in U.S. society is often teasingly called a **flower child.** Some young people today imitate this style and use it as part of their own identity.

   a. Do you know anybody who acts like a flower child?

   b. Is there another name in your community for such a person? Are you such a person?

   c. How are such people treated in your community?

   d. Can this kind of person help your community? How?

   e. List some words that are related to *flower child.*

Before Reading: Ranking

Ranking concepts before reading helps you familiarize yourself with the topic. Giving a reason for your score, even if it is low, prepares you to read. You will know some parts might be harder and you can prepare to read carefully and activate prior knowledge.

On a scale of 1–10, decide how interesting each of these concepts seems to you, and then explain why.

Flower Power

| 10 | 9 | 8 | 7 | 6 | 5 | 4 | 3 | 2 | 1 |

Very Interesting . . . . Not Very Interesting

Why? _____

_____

Universal Love (love thy neighbor)

| 10 | 9 | 8 | 7 | 6 | 5 | 4 | 3 | 2 | 1 |

Very Interesting . . . . Not Very Interesting

Why? _____

_____

Woodstock

| 10 | 9 | 8 | 7 | 6 | 5 | 4 | 3 | 2 | 1 |

Very Interesting . . . . Not Very Interesting

Why? _____

_____

Reading: The U.S. Counterrevolution of the Sixties

After World War II, the economy in the United States was better than it had ever been. People began to have extra money, and they spent it on homes and entertainment. Post-war wealth created a consumer culture in which **materialism** and **consumerism** were increasingly valued. During the 1960s, however, many people began to note that this system favored white, American men and kept minorities and women in lower social positions. The **counterrevolution** was based on a need to organize and protest against the perceived racism and sexism of the **establishment** culture. When young people realized that many aspects of American society were based on fundamental inequality, they openly rebelled against big government, big labor, and middle class values. Even though it has been **romanticized**, the era created some of the most lasting economic, political, and social reform than any other era in U.S. history.

One of the fundamental rifts between the **hippies** and society at large was the hippies' belief in **deception** by the government. Lingering questions about the assassination of John F. Kennedy in 1963, the rise of a nuclear-based military-industrial complex, and conflict both at home (racial tensions in cities) and overseas (Vietnam) created widespread **tensions** and distrust for the way of life that was being modeled by leaders. President Lyndon B. Johnson's "Great Society" meant more government oversight and higher taxes. A negative feeling about (or questioning of) authority began to spread throughout young people. "Don't trust anyone over 30!" became a popular attitude among younger people as they sought an **unprecedented** level of individual freedom from existing social norms. Personal expression, individual potential, freedom from restrictive roles, **interconnectedness** with nature and the environment, and universal love and acceptance became **mantras** of the age.

This took the form of several interrelated movements and pronounced social **activism** in relation to civil rights, free speech, anti-war attitudes, feminism, and environmentalism. Students gathered to protest the war in Vietnam and to educate others at **teach-ins**. "Make love, not war!" was a popular slogan among the youth. College campuses became highly **politicized** centers of protest activity, starting with the Campus Free Speech Movement at Berkeley and spreading rapidly to other schools. For some,

Hippies from the 1960s.

education represented authority, and many students **dropped out**. Some young people left home to live in **communes** in order to get as far away as possible from the traditional social structures. Others chose to be on the move, **hitchhiking** across the country in search of experiences and community.

Men grew beards and wore their hair long as a statement of individual freedom, **non-conformity,** and an act of rebellion. Women began to wear pants instead of skirts or dresses in public as a symbol of breaking out of traditional roles and claiming social equality. Increasing numbers of couples chose to live in relationships outside of marriage, which they thought represented the middle-class "establishment" values that they were fighting against. Other young **"flower children"** were less focused, experimenting with mind-altering drugs in the pursuit of peace and harmony while attempting to access a higher consciousness and to block out the negativity of domestic conflict and overseas war. *Turn on, tune in, drop out* is a counterculture phrase that encouraged others to **detach** from **hierarchy** and embrace change.

During this time, traditional family structures and moral values broke down rapidly, permanently changing American society. They were replaced with new cultural forms that served as a touchstone for the consciousness of the times. The literature of the "beat" writers Jack Kerouac, Ken Keasy, and Tom Wolfe depicted the **restlessness** and **disillusionment** of the hippies, some of whom drifted from coast to coast in search of a new way of life. Psychedelic art became popular for its ability to depict the effects of altered consciousness. A lasting legacy of the hippie era is the music. The rock and roll of Elvis' generation gave way to Beatles rock, the electric stylings of Jimi Hendrix, and the edgy protest lyrics of Bob Dylan. Woodstock, a three-day music festival held in a field in upstate New York, became an icon symbolizing the times.

Responding to Information about the Generation of Flower Power, Universal Love, and Woodstock

An important reading skill is the ability to relate this reading to what you have read, heard, or seen somewhere else, such as a book, poem, cartoon, TV commercial, or song.

Complete one of these activities.

1. How do the teach-ins and protests mentioned in the reading relate to the modern Occupy movement protests?

2. Was there a part in the reading that reminded you of a book, poem, movie, or something else? What was it?

Give a three- to five-minute presentation to the class that shows the relationship between the two. Be sure to give specific details.

Understanding the Reading: Comprehension Check

Fill in the blanks with any word that shows you understood the reading. (The abbreviations in parentheses indicate the part of speech needed: *n = noun; v = verb; a = adjective*.) Check your answers with your classmates and your instructor.

The good post-war economy, in addition to creating a wealthy consumer society,

created a system that valued ① _____ (n). Young people

thought that this system was ② _____ (a), and they were

③ _____ (a) toward the establishment and authority.

Young people pushed for new ④ _____(n). Some

⑤ _____ (v) around the country. Some people still view

the time of the hippies as ⑥ _____ (a), but this is not accurate.

Social activism and protesting often led to ⑦ _____ (n).

Traditional social structures began to ⑧ _____ (v) as

young people ⑨ _____ (v) American society.

Looking at a Novel: *On the Road* by Jack Kerouac

The "beat" generation was the foundation for the counterrevolution and the hippie culture that followed it. One primary theme of the literature of this era is the restlessness and movement typical of a generation of Americans. *On the Road* is a famous U.S. novel written by Jack Kerouac that has come to represent the mood and values of the late 1950s and early 1960s. In the novel, Sal Paradise and his friends hitchhike back and forth across the United States, meeting many new people and experiencing the various aspects of the counterculture. The people he meets are disillusioned with the establishment and are searching for a new way to live their lives.

Read this passage, and then answer the questions.

> It was drizzling and mysterious at the beginning of our journey. I could see that it was all going to be one big saga of mist. 'Whoee!' yelled Dean. 'Here we go!' And he hunched over the wheel and gunned her; he was back in his element, everybody could see that. We were all delighted, we all realized we were leaving confusion and nonsense behind and performing our one and noble function of the time, move. And we moved! We flashed past the mysterious white signs in the night somewhere in New Jersey that say SOUTH (with an arrow) and WEST (with an arrow) and took the south one. New Orleans! It burned in our brains. From the dirty snows of . . . New York…all the way to the greeneries and river smells of old New Orleans at the washed out bottom of America; then west. . . . The purity of the road. The white line in the middle of the highway unrolled and hugged our left front tire as if glued to our groove. (pp. 134–35)

1. Make a list of adjectives to describe the mood in this paragraph.

   _____

   _____

   _____

2. What kind of people are described in the paragraph? Do you think they are like typical U.S. Americans today? Why or why not?

   _____

   _____

   _____

3. Based on details in the paragraph, how prepared do you think Dean was for traveling across the country?

   _____

   _____

   _____

4. Why were they all so pleased to be traveling?

   _____

   _____

   _____

A sign from Route 66 as it passes through New Mexico

Applying What You've Learned from *On the Road:* Traveling Route 66

Toward the end of the novel, Sal and Terry arrive in L.A. via Route 66. This is the name of the most famous road in America, nicknamed "the Main Street of America" and "the Mother Road." Connecting Chicago with Los Angeles, it is 2,448 miles (4,000 km) long and crosses eight states and three time zones. Prior to interstate freeway travel, this two-lane highway was a primary means of crossing the United States by car. To many people, it represents the romanticism and freedom of those who chose to make cross-country trips to start a new life or to enjoy the freedom of seeing a different part of the country.

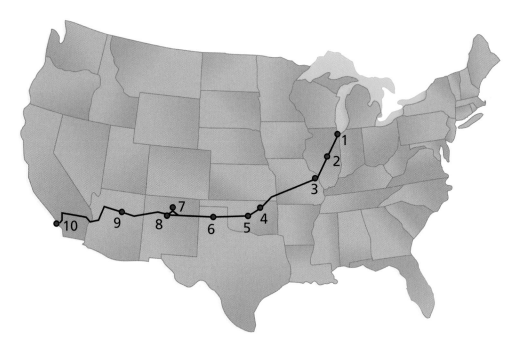

Look at the map of Route 66 and trace its path from east to west. Although Route 66 crosses through mostly small towns, it also goes through 10 major U.S. cities. List the major cities. Use an outside reference to help you.

1.

2.

3.

4.

5.

6.

7.

8.

9.

10.

Using an encyclopedia from a library or information from the Internet, look up information about each of these cities and the states in which they are located.

- What are the main attractions in each city?

  _____

  _____

- What is the population?

  _____

  _____

- What is the climate?

  _____

  _____

- What is the geography/landscape like?

  _____

  _____

- What do most people in the area do for a living?

  _____

  _____

Work with a partner to discuss what major changes in population and topography you can find by tracing Route 66 from east to west.

LANGUAGE FOCUS: Using Discourse Markers in Paragraph-Level Description and Narration

Travel literature is very popular in the United States. People enjoy talking about and listening to others tell stories about where they have been and what they experienced there. Stories are told in the simple past tense, but speakers often switch to what is referred to as "historical present" because it has the effect of making the story more vivid for the listener. Good storytellers also use discourse markers to help with cohesion or emotion. Discourse markers can be particles or connectives. Particles are usually placed at the beginning or end of a statement. Connectives "connect" two ideas or thoughts. This helps the listener to understand how the events relate to each other in time and space and understand how the speaker feels. Look at the examples of discourse markers and how they are used to narrate.

Particles	Connectives
oh—"Oh, we had a great time on our road trip!"	*(at) first*—"First, we packed our bags."
well—"Well, I was not prepared for what happened next."	*then*—"Then, we tried to hitchhike, but nobody would pick us up."
now—"Now, I had been studying maps for months."	*after that*—"After that, we decided to buy a bus ticket."
you see—"To get to the Rockies from the midwest, I had to drive through Kansas, you see."	*so*—"The busses were full, so we decided to try the train."
I mean—"I mean, there was nothing in that desert for miles and miles."	*because*—"That didn't work because the train didn't go where we wanted to go."
Right?—"So then, I realize that it is a holiday and there is no bus, right?"	*and*—"And then we found out that the main freeway out of town was blocked due to road construction."
You know? "The midwest is flat as a pancake, you know?"	*but*—"But that was supposed to end the next day, so we decided to postpone the journey."
	Or—"It was either that, or spend time sitting around being stuck somewhere else."

Think about an experience that you have had "on the road" (traveling).

1. Make a list of things that happened.

2. Add discourse markers to connect the events and express emotions.

3. Tell your story to the class.

LINK TO TODAY: Earth Day and Environmentalism—Reduce, Reuse, Recycle

The first Earth Day was proposed by John McConnell and celebrated in San Francisco on March 21, 1970—the first day of spring. Shortly thereafter, Senator Gaylord Nelson organized student war activists to protest the effects of a large oil spill that had wreaked havoc in Santa Barbara, California. His goal was to gain national attention for the cause of environmental awareness. On April 22, 1970, 20 million Americans organized and demonstrated coast to coast for environmental protection against the deterioration caused by pollution, toxic waste, pesticides, and deforestation. Organizers grew the movement and it quickly spread across the United States. It went international in 1990 and is now a global phenomenon organized by the Earth Day Network. It is celebrated by an estimated 200 million people in 175 countries and recognized by the United Nations, which designated April 22 as International Mother Earth Day in 2009. Large-scale environmental awareness led to the creation of the United States Environmental Protection Agency and the passage of the Clean Air, Clean Water, and Endangered Species Acts by Congress.

Today, local communities celebrate by organizing programs for establishing recycling programs, teaching composting, planting trees and/or gardens, or picking up trash. Some people use the day as an opportunity to lobby for further awareness and circulate petitions for stronger governmental action. Worldwide observances have included bell ringings, parades, global drumming circles, and theme parties. Vegetarian eating is also promoted as a lifestyle choice that uses fewer resources and protects the environment. It is not uncommon to see "Meatless Mondays" in cafeterias. Many people who cannot grow their own food have begun to subscribe to organic produce farms and to shop at organic food chains. For more information on Earth Day and environmental awareness, visit www.earthday.org.

Fast Facts

- A Greenpeace International study published in 2011 indicates that the data centers used to house virtual data consume two percent of all global energy and that this rate grows by 12 percent per year. The electricity demands of "cloud" computing and the companies that host it rely on coal power for between 50–80 percent of their energy needs.[1]

---

[1] Cook, Gary and Jodie Van Horn. (2011). *How dirty is your data? A look at the energy choices that power cloud computing.* Amsterdam: Greenpeace International. www.greenpeace.org/international/Global/international/publications/climate/2011/Cool%20IT/dirty-data-report-greenpeace.pdf.

- The United States Environmental Protection Agency estimates that each American uses an average of 100 gallons of water a day, that 5–10 percent of American homes have water leaks that waste an average of 90 gallons a day, and that at least 36 states are projecting water shortages by the year 2013.[2]

- A March 2011 update to a United Nations report showed that the U.S. and the former Soviet Union were the two largest producers of hazardous waste in the world in 2009.[3]

- The U.S. Environmental Protection Agency has identified 25 states that have enacted laws for the reuse or recycling of end-of-life electronics such as televisions, cell phones, and printers. The Consumer Electronics Association (CEA) estimated in 2008 that there were about 24 electronic products in each American household.[4]

Find and read two newspaper, magazine, or Internet articles, one with positive aspects of environmentalism and one detailing the negative aspects. Summarize each article. Then write a short paragraph about your personal conclusions.

positive aspects of environmentalism

_____

_____

_____

_____

negative aspects of environmentalism

_____

_____

_____

_____

my personal conclusion(s) about environmentalism in the United States

_____

_____

_____

_____

[2] U.S. Environmental Protection Agency. (February 2012). Water sense. www.epa.gov/WaterSense/resources/facts.html.

[3] U.S. Statistics Division. (March 2011). Environemental indicators. http://unstats.un.org/unsd/environment/hazardous.htm.

[4] U.S. Environmental Protection Agency. (2011). ecycling. www.epa.gov/osw/conserve/materials/ecycling/.

Putting It All Together

Reflect, and then write your ideas about these questions. Then discuss them in a group.

1. What surprised me most about the information on the counterrevolution in the U.S.?

   _____

   _____

2. What does this information help me to understand about modern U.S. American life?

   _____

   _____

3. Does this information change my opinions about U.S. American values and attitudes? How?

   _____

   _____

4. Can people in other countries learn something from the experiences U.S. Americans had with the counterrevolution?

   _____

   _____

5. What will I tell people if they ask me about hippies of the 1960s?

   _____

   _____

6. What positive changes can other countries make regarding environmentalism? Should they make any changes at all?

   _____

   _____

6

The U.S. in the Cold War Era

Defending Democracy from McCarthy to Vietnam

President Johnson greets U.S. troops in Vietnam in 1966. (Courtesy DoD Visual Information Record Center.)

The events in this unit focus on foreign policy and political and ideological issues centering around a belief in the primacy of democracy from the 1950s through the 1970s. During those decades, the U.S. was entangled in a "cold war" with the Soviet Union and actively engaged in wars in Korea and Vietnam.

Net Surfers

To learn more about the time period covered in this unit, search for these names, words, and phrases on the Internet.

Berlin airlift	ROTC
Cold War	Senator Joseph McCarthy
GI Bill	veterans
Marshall Plan	Vietnam Veterans Memorial
the Red Scare 1945 to 1954	Vietnam Women's Memorial Foundation

★ ──────────────────────────── ★

Presidential Suite

Harry S Truman (D) 1945–1953
Dwight D. Eisenhower (R) 1953–1961
John F. Kennedy (D) 1961–1963
Lyndon B. Johnson (D) 1963–1969
Richard M. Nixon (R) 1969–1974
Gerald R. Ford (R) 1974–1977

★ ──────────────────────────── ★

On TV

All in the Family
China Beach
M*A*S*H

★ ──────────────────────────── ★

Music Box

"Fortunate Son"—Credence Clearwater Revival
"Where Have All the Flowers Gone?"—Pete Seeger

At the Movies

Apocalypse Now
Born on the Fourth of July
Coming Home
Full Metal Jacket
Platoon
The Deer Hunter
Thirteen Days

Preparing to Read about Defending Democracy from McCarthy to Vietnam

Write some thoughts about these topics, and then discuss them with your classmates.

1. The politics of communism and socialism

   a. What do you already know about communism and socialism?

   _____

   b. What are some of the benefits of living in a communist and socialist society?

   _____

   _____

   c. What are some of the drawbacks of living in such a society?

   _____

   _____

   d. What kinds of attitudes do you think U.S. Americans have about communism and socialism?

   _____

   _____

2. the politics of democracy

    a. What do you already know about free markets and democracy?

    _____

    b. What are some of the benefits of living in a democratic society?

    _____

    _____

    c. What are some of the drawbacks of living in such a society?

    _____

    _____

    d. What kinds of attitudes do you think U.S. Americans have about democracy?

    _____

    _____

3. ideological stances

    a. What types of political ideology are promoted in your family's home country?

    _____

    _____

    b. Do you feel strongly about any political ideology?

    _____

    _____

Learning New Vocabulary about the U.S. in the Cold War Era

Although this is a long list of words to learn, these words will be helpful to understanding the reading. Preview the vocabulary and definitions, and refer to the list as needed.

brink (n) edge

Cold War (n) a war of beliefs between East and West, represented by the "superpowers" of the former Soviet Socialist Republics (USSR) and the United States. The cold war ended with the fall of the Berlin Wall in 1989 and the collapse of the Soviet Union.

communism (n) a political belief that promotes state control of most resources and public distribution of funds in society

democracy (n) a political belief that promotes private control of most resources and private distribution of funds in society

riot (n) disorder or uprising

scorn (n) extreme dislike or disapproval

sentiment (n) feelings

socialism (n) economic system that promotes production and distribution of materials owned by the government

standoff (n) an argument in which neither side will give in

sympathy (n) having positive feelings or understanding about something or someone

veteran (n) a person who has served the U.S. in a war

witch hunt (n) search for people whose political or religious activities are dangerous

to assassinate (v) to murder a famous person—often a political leader—by surprise attack

to be associated with (v) to have connections with or to be related to

to bolster (v) to strengthen

to draft (v) to force someone to fight in a war

to extend (v) to go beyond the original action or state

to monitor (v) to keep track of

to overthrow (v) to take over another country's leadership

domestic (adj) at home; in politics refers to within the United States

suspected (adj) something that is thought but not proven

Talking about New Words and Concepts

Take some time to think and talk about new ideas associated with the vocabulary. Then use your understanding of the new vocabulary to discuss each set of questions with a partner.

1. **Communism** and **democracy** are political ideologies. An **ideology** shapes the thinking and the activities of large groups of people, such as a religious group or a government. Human beings group themselves based on ideologies.

   a. Explain your understanding of democracy.

   b. Explain your understanding of communism.

   c. Are ideologies helpful or harmful to human beings? Both? Explain how.

   d. List some words that are related to *democracy* and *communism*.

2. A **riot** is caused when a large group of people becomes violent. This can be due to premeditated protesting, as was the case in Los Angeles in 1994 when members of various ethnic groups protested the verdict in the case of police brutality against Rodney King. Or, it can happen somewhat accidentally when large crowds of people become excited at or about concerts or sporting events.

   a. Have there ever been riots in your community or city that you remember? What was the reason for the riot?

   b. Have you ever been involved in a riot? If so, was it intentional or accidental?

   c. Do you think rioting is an effective way to demonstrate for what you believe in?

   d. List some words that are related to *riot.*

3. A **witch hunt** is a term used when people in power seek those who do not believe the same way they do and cause those people bodily or emotional harm. Today, this is mostly a political event. However, in the 17th century, anyone who was not liked in the community or broke the rules in some way could be accused of being a witch by his/her neighbors. A public trial would be held that often involved the accused "proving" that he/she was not a witch by performing an act such as walking on hot coals. If the suspected person did not get burned, this was proof that the victim was not human and, therefore, was indeed a witch.

    a. Has anything similar to a witch hunt ever happened in your community's history? If so, explain as many details as you can.

    b. Could something like a witch hunt happen in your community today? In the future?

    c. Have you noticed any examples of such behavior in smaller forms?

    d. What do you think causes people to accuse others?

    e. What can you do to help make sure that people are not falsely accused?

    f. List some words that are related to *witch hunt.*

4. When a planned attack against a public official or leader occurs and that person dies, it is referred to as an **assassination.** Four U.S. presidents have been assassinated: Abraham Lincoln, James Garfield, William McKinley, and John F. Kennedy. There were assassination attempts against Presidents Gerald Ford and Ronald Reagan. In addition, Martin Luther King, Jr., and Senator Robert F. Kennedy were both assassinated in 1968.

    a. Can you think of other world or local leaders who were assassinated? Who? Do you know who did it and why?

    b. Is it justifiable to assassinate a leader because you do not believe in him/her? Why or why not?

    c. Is it justifiable to assassinate a leader who is harming the people? Why or why not?

    d. List some words that are related to *assassination.*

Before Reading: Using a Graphic Organizer

Graphic organizers are used to collect and represent data or details in a visual way. You can use graphic organizers before reading to analyze the main concept or topic. Doing this will make understanding the reading easier.

Use the graphic organizer to analyze the concept of democracy that will be central to the reading.

How do I define democracy?

What does democracy look like? How do I know when I see it?

Democracy

What are some examples of democracy?

What is my experience with democracy?

Reading: The U.S. in the Cold War Era

The importance of **democracy** as an ideal influenced both **domestic** and foreign activities in the 1950s and 1960s. Overseas, the U.S. dedicated itself to stopping the "red plague" of **communism**. Driven by the belief in the "domino effect," which stated that if one country fell to communism, then the countries near it would fall also, the U.S. sent money and military aid to post–World War II Europe and Asia to **bolster** democratic governments. In Europe, the U.S. put the Marshall Plan into place to help West Germany with rebuilding after World War II. As part of the treaty to end World War II, both Germany and the capital city of Berlin were divided into four occupation zones that were held by England, France, the United States, and Russia. While the first three combined their zones under a democratic umbrella, Russia pulled its zone into communist rule, lowering a so-called "iron curtain" that divided Germany into two countries—East and West—until the fall of the Berlin Wall in 1989. During one difficult winter, the U.S. flew multiple plane loads of food, blankets, and supplies into West Berlin so that the city did not fall to the nearby Soviet occupation zone. A similar situation between North and South Korea led to U.S. involvement in the Korean War from 1950–1953.

The White House stands as a symbol of democracy. (Courtesy DoD Visual Information Record Center.)

U.S. soldiers observe
the Berlin Wall
from the West
German side, 1984.
(Courtesy DoD
Visual Information
Record Center.)

At home, Wisconsin Senator Joseph McCarthy was busy leading an anti-communist **witch hunt** in Washington, after Alger Hiss, a State Department official, was accused and found guilty of spying for the Soviets. This witch hunt was aimed at anyone and everyone who was thought to have ties to or **sympathies** for the Communist Party and included many famous authors, playwrights, directors, and actors. The U.S. Communist Party was required to give a list of its members to the government, and those who had been **associated with** communism in other countries were not allowed to live in the United States. Communism was thought to be such a threat to the U.S. that neighbors and co-workers **monitored** and reported each other to the government for **suspected** Communist activities. Meanwhile, the nation refocused its efforts on math and science in order to win a growing nuclear arms race and a space race that landed U.S. Apollo astronauts on the moon in 1969.

While much of the threat of communism was far removed from America, the tiny Caribbean island of Cuba, just off the Florida shore, was under a **socialist** government. This threat prompted the Bay of Pigs Invasion in 1961—an unsuccessful attempt by the United States to **overthrow** Cuba's communist-influenced government. Afterward, the Soviets began to build bases for nuclear missiles that were capable of reaching the United States. (The U.S. had already placed similar missiles in Turkey that could easily reach Moscow.) The result was the October 1962 Cuban Missile Crisis. This thirteen-

A U.S. Army tank maneuvers in downtown Saigon, Vietnam, in 1966. (Courtesy DoD Visual Information Record Center.)

day **standoff** between the United States and the Soviet Union brought the world to the **brink** of nuclear war. The Soviet Union backed off from putting missiles in Cuba, and later, the U.S. (quietly) removed missiles from Turkey.

Vietnam was another country divided along political lines, with the North under Soviet and Chinese communist influence and the South wishing to remain democratic. Ideologically bound to help struggling South Vietnam, both President Dwight D. Eisenhower and President John F. Kennedy sent "military advisors" to the area. By the time Kennedy was **assassinated** on November 22, 1963, more than 15,000 U.S. American soldiers were stationed in Vietnam. President Lyndon B. Johnson, who became president after Kennedy's death, **extended** this effort by ordering U.S. forces to bomb the Northern Vietcong for attacking U.S. ships off South Vietnam. The Tonkin Gulf Resolution passed by Congress in August 1964 gave the president the authority to act in Vietnam without officially declaring war. By March 1965, 184,000 U.S. American troops were fighting in an unofficial war in Vietnam.

Much of the population did not support being involved in an Asian civil war, and war protests spread all across the nation, especially on college campuses. Building on public **sentiment**, Richard Nixon was elected president in 1968 on a platform of withdrawing the troops from Vietnam. However, the number of deployed soldiers kept growing, and in 1969, 100,000 people marched in Washington, DC, to protest. As more and more young men were **drafted** to fight, many left for Canada while others burned

Visitors pay tribute at the Vietnam Veterans Memorial. (Courtesy DoD Visual Information Record Center.)

draft cards and U.S. flags in the streets. Protests became more vocal and violent clashes began to result. In 1970, at Kent State University in Ohio, four students were killed and several wounded when a few members of the U.S. National Guard shot into a crowd of war protesters. The U.S. would not officially leave Vietnam until 1975.

Because so many Americans were against the war, soldiers who fought in Vietnam came home to **scorn** and anger compared to the hero's welcome for soldiers of previous U.S. wars. The traumas these **veterans** experienced in Vietnam caused physical and emotional harm that left many unable to work and still have lasting social effects that are felt to this day. Homelessness among returning soldiers became a new social issue. In 1982, the U.S. government recognized the service of these veterans by building the Vietnam Veterans Memorial in Washington, DC. The typical picture of the Vietnam veteran is of a young male. However, more than one-quarter of a million women also served voluntarily on the front lines of the war in military hospitals and offices. Women veterans who served in Vietnam were honored with their own statue in 1993.

Responding to Information about Defending Democracy from McCarthy to Vietnam

In the last two units, you made connections between the reading and your life and between the reading and other materials. Another connection skill that is important is to be able to make connections between the reading and the world. These connections do not need to involve world powers or large countries but may be small events close to home. The events in the reading can remind us of things happening at our school, in our neighborhoods, or in our cities.

Complete these activities.

1. Does some of the information in the reading remind you of things that are happening in the world?

   _____

   _____

2. Write a paragraph about them on a separate piece of paper.

Understanding the Reading: Comprehension Check

Write a short answer to each question.

1. Describe the kind of competition that took place between the United States and the Soviet Union during the Cold War.

   _____

   _____

2. Why did U.S. Americans call communism the "red plague"?

   _____

   _____

3. How did the United States try to stop Communism from spreading in foreign countries?

   _____

   _____

4. Describe the domino effect.

   _____

   _____

5. What differences are there in the way that Presidents Kennedy and Johnson responded to the crisis in Vietnam?

   _____

   _____

Applying Your Understanding to Put Events in Historical Order

Using your knowledge of the progression of historical events before, during, and after the Vietnam War, put the following twelve statements in the correct order.

___ Presidents Dwight D. Eisenhower and John F. Kennedy send "military advisors" to Vietnam to help South Vietnam remain stable.

___ Congress passes the Tonkin Gulf Resolution, allowing President Johnson to officially order bombing raids against North Vietnam.

___ Vietnam veterans are scorned and disrespected when they return from the war.

___ Protesting at Kent State University in Ohio leaves four students dead and nine wounded.

___ Richard M. Nixon is elected president of the United States.

___ World War II ends, leaving two superpowers in the world with opposing economic systems and ideologies.

___ The Vietnam Veterans Memorial is built and dedicated.

___ The draft threatens many young men, and some leave the U.S. for Canada.

___ 100,000 people march in Washington, D.C., to show the government what they think about the Vietnam conflict.

___ The United States sends money and military aid to areas of the world threatened by communism.

___ John F. Kennedy is assassinated. Vice President Lyndon B. Johnson is sworn in as president.

On Board the *General Nelson M. Walker*—The Vietnam Graffiti Project

The Vietnam Graffiti Project (VGP) is a collection of stories and graffiti by Vietnam soldiers who were transported to and from the war on the *General Nelson M. Walker* transport ship in 1997. To read some of their stories and to see some of their personal artwork and other artifacts, visit the Graffiti Project at www.vietnamgraffiti.com/stories.

Looking at a Novel (Collection): *The Things They Carried* by Tim O'Brien

The Things They Carried is a collection of pieces that forms one story about a platoon of American soldiers serving in the Vietnam War. It's about the items they had with them, such as malaria medicine and love letters, as well as the emotions they carried with them all the time. Although the book is considered a work of fiction, some people believe that some of the content is based on the author's life. Tim O'Brien was in the U.S. Army during the Vietnam War. The book has been read by millions of people and is often required reading in classrooms.

Read this passage.

> They carried all the emotional baggage of men who might die. Grief, terror, love, longing—those were intangibles, but the intangibles had their own mass and specific gravity, they had tangible weight. They carried shameful memories. They carried the common secret of cowardice barely restrained, the instinct to run or freeze or hide, and in many respects this was the heaviest burden of all, for it could never be put down, it required perfect balance and perfect posture. They carried their reputations. They carried the soldier's greatest fear, which was the fear of blushing. Men killed, and died, because they were embarrassed not to. It was what had brought them to the war in the first place, nothing positive, no dreams of glory or honor, just to avoid the blush of dishonor. They died so as not to die of embarrassment. They crawled into tunnels and walked point and advanced under fire. Each morning, despite the unknowns, they made their legs move. They endured. They kept humping. They did not submit to the obvious alternative, which was simply to close the eyes and fall. So easy really. Go limp and tumble to the ground and let the muscles unwind and not speak and not budge until your buddies picked you up and lifted you into the chopper that would roar and dip its nose and carry you off to the world. A mere matter of falling, yet no one ever fell. It was not courage, exactly; the object was not valor. Rather, they were too frightened to be cowards. (pp. 20–21)

LANGUAGE FOCUS: Using Parallelism for Cohesion in Paragraph-Length Description

The way that O'Brien describes the soldiers uses a series of similarly structured sentences that give the reader an idea about their physical characteristics and their collective personality traits without relying on lists of adjectives. Read the statements that he makes about the soldiers. Based on your interpretation of the statements, list adjectives that describe the soldiers physically and emotionally.

Physically	Emotionally

1. Re-read the paragraph. What sentences are structured similarly? How many times in one paragraph? This kind of repetition is called parallelism and it is one way that an author can achieve focused paragraph length description of a person, place, thing, or event.

2. Think about a group of people you know. Complete the chart.

Physical Traits	Emotional Characteristics

3. Write a descriptive paragraph about them using O'Brien's model. Address collective traits and characteristics and use parallelism.

LINK TO TODAY: The U.S. Military Today—Who Wears the Uniform?

The U.S. military ended the draft in 1972, so today's force is comprised entirely of volunteers. The Army makes up the biggest percentage (about 38 percent) of the military followed by the Air Force and Navy (about 22 percent each), the Marines (about 14 percent), and the Coast Guard (about 3 percent). According to information from the Defense Manpower Data Center, the face of the U.S. military's enlisted ranks is fairly representative of the U.S. youth population at large.[1] About half of the non-officers currently in uniform are between 22–30 years of age. Most are middle class. Approximately 74 percent are white, and 26 percent represent minorities. One in seven is female, and half of all enlistees are married. A disproportionate number of recruits come from rural areas. The South and Intermountain West are highly represented. A wide variety of religions is found among enlistees. In addition to U.S. Americans, about 40,000 non-citizen green card holders are enlisted military personnel.

Many young people join the military right after high school at age 18; others choose to go to college first and then enter the service as officers. Therefore, it is not uncommon to see military recruiters at high schools and on college campuses, although they have been banned from some institutions. Many join the military for job training and/or money to attend college through a law called the *Montgomery GI Bill*. This education program has been available to returning service-men and women since World War II to help veterans further their training and education in civilian fields. Since September 11, 2001, the financial incentives have expanded and a new policy allows some veterans to transfer the benefit to their spouse or dependent child. Universities, community colleges, and vocational training schools are expecting a large increase in the number of veteran students on campus due to wars in Iraq and Afghanistan.

Another option that combines job training with college credit is ROTC (Reserve Officer Training Corps). In ROTC, freshmen and sophomores can try the military. There is no obligation for them to be there; rather, they are learning whether this is something they might want to pursue as a career in the future. Juniors, seniors, and even some graduate students who participate have made a four- to ten-year commitment to the U.S. military and will enter as officers when they graduate from school. They are eligible to receive scholarships and a tax-free, monthly stipend while they participate. You may see them in uniform as they go about their job training, education, and family life.

[1] U.S. Department of Defense. (2011). Service member demographic data. http://open.dodlive.mil/data-gov/demographics/.

Fast Facts

A study by the U.S. Congress shows that more than twice as much money was spent on defense outlays during the World War II era than at any other before or after.

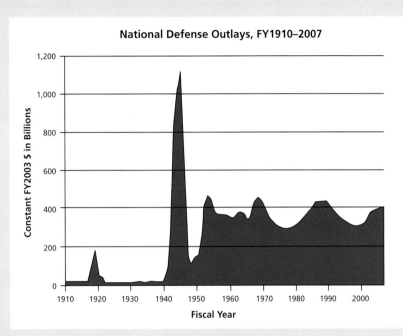

National Defense Outlays, FY1910–2007

Courtesy of
Congressional
Research Service—
U. S. Government

- An academic study published in 2011 found that the U.S. public was more likely to support military intervention when the media depicted the campaign as revolving around the prevention of losses rather than when it was reported as revolving around the securing of gains.[2]

- GI bills provide education and support for war veterans. In 2009, President Obama approved a series of changes to the Post 9/11 GI Bill that provides benefits to more members of the military as well as the spouses and dependents of veterans, and includes a broader scope of post-secondary training and study.[3]

- The U.S. Bureau of Labor Statistics reports that the 2010 unemployment rate for Gulf War–Era II veterans (since September 2001) was 11.5 percent. The jobless rate for veterans of all eras combined was 8.7 percent, compared with 9.4 percent for non-veterans.[4]

---

[2] Perla, Hector. (2011). Explaining public support for the use of military force: The impact of reference point framing and Prospective decision making. *International Organization Journal* 65, 139–67. http://ucsc.academia.edu/HectorPerla/Papers/139832/Explaining_Public_Support_for_the_Use_of_Military_Force_The_Impact_of_Reference_Point_Framing_and_Prospective_Decision_Making.

[3] U.S. Department of Veteran's Affairs. (2012). The Post 9/11 GI-Bill. www.gibill.va.gov/benefits/post_911_gibill/index.html.

[4] U.S. Bureau of Labor. (March 2011). *Employment situation of veterans.* www.bls.gov/news.release/vet.nr0.htm.

Find and read two newspaper, magazine, or Internet articles, one with positive aspects of military service and one detailing the negative aspects. Summarize each article. Then write a short paragraph about your personal conclusions.

positive aspects of military service

_____

_____

_____

_____

negative aspects of military service

_____

_____

_____

_____

my personal conclusion(s) about military service in the United States

_____

_____

_____

_____

Putting It All Together

Reflect, and then write your ideas about these questions. Then discuss them in a group.

1. What surprised me most about the information on the Cold War era?

   _____

   _____

2. What does this information help me to understand about modern U.S. American life?

   _____

   _____

3. Does this information change my opinions about U.S. American values and attitudes? How?

   _____

   _____

4. Can people in other countries learn something from the experiences U.S. Americans had with the Cold War, McCarthy, and the Vietnam War?

   _____

   _____

5. What will I tell people if they ask me about democracy in the United States?

   _____

   _____

6. What positive changes can other countries make regarding decisions to fight wars? Should they make any changes at all?

   _____

   _____

7 The U.S. Value Wars

Equal Rights, Civil Liberties, and the Moral Majority

Wall art reflecting some of the values popular in the 1970s; words here from John Lennon's song.

The 1960s were highlighted by civil rights at home and fighting overseas. The civil rights movement of the 1960s led to an examination of other types of equality, particularly women's rights in the 1970s. These issues led people to question the notions of home and family that lasted through the Reagan era (the 1980s).

Net Surfers

To learn more about the time period covered in this unit, search for these names, words, and phrases on the Internet.

Equal Rights Amendment	conservatism
National Women's Hall of Fame	Moral Majority
National Women's History Project	equal access
Ms. Foundation for Women	trickle down economics
Title IX	latchkey children
American Civil Liberties Union	Yuppies
hate crime legislation	Silicon Valley
Christian Coalition	dot.com bubble
liberalism	Sandra Day O'Connor

Presidential Suite

Richard M. Nixon (R) 1969–1974
Gerald R. Ford (R) 1974–1977
James Earl (Jimmy) Carter, Jr. (D) 1977–1981
Ronald W. Reagan (R) 1981–1989

On TV

All in the Family
The Mary Tyler Moore Show
Sanford and Son
That '70s Show

Music Box

"I Am Woman"—Helen Reddy
"9 to 5"—Dolly Parton
"Another Day in Paradise"—Phil Collins
"Material Girl"—Madonna
"Winds of Change"—Scorpions

At the Movies

Saturday Night Fever
Billie Beat Bobby
9 to 5
ET—The Extra Terrestrial
Home Alone

Preparing to Read about the U.S. Value Wars

Write some thoughts about these topics, and then discuss them with your classmates.

1. social gap between rich and poor

   a. How is wealth defined in your family's home country?

   _____

   b. How big is the gap between rich and poor in that country? What has prevented or contributed to that?

   _____

   _____

   c. What types of results—positive and negative—have occurred due to unequal distribution of wealth?

   _____

   _____

2. raising future generations

    a. Whose responsibility is it to care for and raise children in your family's home country?

    _____

    b. What types of childcare are available for working parents there?

    _____

    c. What is a common philosophy about having children in daycare or childcare while one or both parents work?

    _____

    _____

    d. What are the benefits and drawbacks of daycare or nannies, etc.?

    _____

    _____

3. public values

    a. Who determines public laws and values in your family's home country?

    _____

    _____

    b. What are the sources of conflict between liberal and conservative public opinion there?

    _____

    _____

    c. Should people bring their personal values into public settings?

    _____

    _____

Learning New Vocabulary about the U.S. Value Wars

Although this is a long list of words to learn, these words will be helpful to understanding the reading. Preview the vocabulary and definitions, and refer to the list as needed.

backlash (n) strong reaction to something

climate (n) condition or set of attitudes about the events one is surrounded by

conservatism (n) philosophy or belief that likes tradition and opposes change

honorifics (n) titles given to people to show respect (Dr., Mr., Ms.)

liberalism (n) a philosophy or attitude that is generally opposed to tradition and favors change toward a freer or less restricted society

outsourcing (n) the practice of moving jobs from one country to another country that has lower costs of doing business

parity (n) equality in number or amount

proponent (n) supporter; somebody who pushes something forward

retiree (n) person who is no longer working due to age, a pensioner

upsurge (n) large increase in something

to be caught up in (v) to be in the middle of or heavily involved in something

to coin (v) to create a new word or term in a language

to dovetail (v) to fit together closely or logically

to eliminate (v) to get rid of or stop something

to fall short (v) to not make a goal or not have enough; to be inadequate

to migrate (v) to move, usually in search of better weather or better jobs

to ratify (v) to approve; in the U.S. government, the act of individual state representatives voting

disadvantaged (adj) not having advantages; being behind others

landmark (adj) marking an important event or turning point in history

sweeping (adj) quick and large-scale change

underperforming (adj) not doing well; not at the level that something should be

unionized (adj) protected by a trade union that represents employees against the interests of management

unsupervised (adj) not being watched over or taken care of

Talking about New Words and Concepts

Take some time to think and talk about new ideas associated with the vocabulary. Then use your understanding of the new vocabulary to discuss each set of questions with a partner.

1. Languages have different ways to talk about people and show the relationship or distance between them. Many languages have a formal and an informal *you* form. Some languages use different vocabulary or word endings depending on the age, social distance, and respect conveyed between the speakers. Most languages rely on a combination of these elements. Other languages such as English rely mostly on forms of address (linguists refer to these as **honorifics**). For example, Mr. William Jones can be called in polite/distanced speech *Mr. Jones*, in informal/close speech *William*, or in family/friend speech *Will* or *Bill*. Think about how speakers of your native language show respect/disrespect to the people they are speaking with.

   a. Do you think there is a relationship between the way different languages show respect and the way relationships between various people function in different societies? Give examples from your native language and other languages you know.

   b. Can you think of ways that people can use patterns of addressing people as tools to show equality? Dominance? Subordination?

   c. How important do you think it is to be familiar with various forms of address of the language you are learning?

   d. List some words that are related to *honorifics*.

2. When there is not enough of something to reach a goal, we say that something **fell short.** This can be used concretely, as in money or resources, or it can be used abstractly in the sense of something not reaching its full potential, such as an idea or a plan.

   a. Can you think of a time in your life when you or an effort you were involved in fell short?

   b. How did it make you feel? Did you try again?

   c. If something is important to citizens, such as passing a new law, how important is it for them to keep trying? Why?

   d. Can efforts that fall short still be important in a country's history, even if they do not succeed?

   e. List some words that are related to *falling short.*

3. An important event in a nation or an organization's history is called a **landmark** event. In this case, it is used as an adjective to describe the event. It may help you to know that as a noun, a landmark also refers to a famous place. Both refer to something out of the ordinary or special that marks a place in space or time.

   a. What are some landmark events in your country's history? Explain their importance.

   b. What are some landmark events in your personal life? Explain their importance.

   c. List some words that are related to *landmark.*

4. The word *climate* usually refers to the weather. For example, the desert has a dry climate. The word can also refer to your surroundings in general. U.S. Americans often talk about the **political climate** when discussing events that have an effect on the feel of their everyday lives. For example, the Cold War climate of the 1950s and 1960s made U.S. Americans feel uneasy and unsettled, whereas the climate of economic boom in the 1990s tended to make people feel more secure.

   a. How would you describe the current political climate in places you have lived or are living? What are the reasons for this climate? How does it make people feel?

   b. Is there anything that could make this climate change rapidly? If so, what?

   c. Do you feel comfortable with the current political climate you find yourself in? Why or why not?

   d. List any words that are related to *political climate.*

5. An attitude of opposition toward liberal trends and increased diversity in society is generally labeled **conservatism.** Although this attitude can be found in U.S. citizens from all walks of life, it tends to show up in groups of people who are wealthier than average, Caucasian, and/or fundamentally religious. One interesting cultural/political dynamic to note is that such people tend to be attracted to the beliefs of the Republican Party, although this is changing somewhat as the agendas of both parties become more and more similar as time progresses.

   a. Is there a distinct opposition between conservatism and liberalism in your community? If so, who belongs to each of these groups and what issues are they concerned with?

   b. Do you think that people who subscribe to conservatism have something to gain from it? What? How about people who subscribe to liberalism?

   c. What is to be lost by those who hold exclusively to either one of these viewpoints?

   d. List any words that are related to *conservatism.*

Before Reading: Making Predictions

A good strategy to use when you are making predictions is adding a reason why you are making the prediction. [It can be based on anything you have seen in the unit (photos, text, etc.) and there is no right or wrong answer.] Making hypotheses (reasonable guess) and supporting opinions (with evidence) makes students better readers and writers.

Without looking at the reading and using your discussion and new vocabulary, make a list of five ideas you expect to appear in the reading. Next to your idea, write a reason why you think each idea will be included.

1. _____

   because_____

2. _____

   because_____

3. _____

   because_____

4. _____

   because_____

5. _____

   because_____

Reading: The U.S. Value Wars

At the beginning of the 1970s, the United States was **caught up in** violent protests against the still-raging Vietnam War and feeling the effects of continued racism despite gains made during the civil rights movement of the previous decade. Concerns about energy and the environment added to these worries. Additionally, women were busy organizing to claim the full benefits and rights that they fought for during the suffrage movement in the 1920s and earned as major contributors to the victory in World War II. Partly due to the awareness created by psychologist Betty Friedan's book *The Feminist Mystique** in the 1960s, and partly due to economic need, females became a larger percentage of the employed. However, statistics showed that those women were earning 58.2 percent of what men earned. In 1970, to mark the 50th anniversary of the suffrage movement and the constitutional right to vote, marches were organized in support of the Equal Rights Amendment (ERA), which would have made discrimination on the basis of sex and unequal pay illegal per federal law.

Awareness fed the 1972 launch of Gloria Steinem and Letty Cottin Pogrebin's *Ms.***—a feminist magazine. In 1973, the U.S. Supreme Court reached a **landmark** decision in the case of *Roe* v. *Wade,* making it illegal for any individual state to deny women a legal abortion during the first three months of pregnancy, an issue that remains a hot button on the public agenda. In the same year, Billie Jean King won her famous tennis match against Bobby Riggs, paving the way for Title IX, which guaranteed **parity** for women's sports teams in schools. The title made it possible for female athletes to earn college scholarships and play in professional leagues. In 1977, the First

---

**The Feminist Mystique* was based on in-depth interviews and statistical analyses of information obtained in research on U.S. American housewives. Its main thesis was that women were bored, frustrated, and unfulfilled as housewives. Friedan's proposed solution to these findings was more opportunities for women to work outside the home lead to self-discovery and a better understanding of their own identity. Many viewed these ideas as a threat to the family and the right of women to be valued as wives and mothers.

***Ms.* magazine is a feminist publication dedicated to expanding awareness of the female self and feminism. *Ms.* is a relatively new form of address in U.S. American English. It is a combination of *Mrs.* and *Miss* titles, which show marital status and are linked to age/respect. *Ms.* was **coined** as a **form of address** or **honorific** because men's marital status is not indicated by *Mr.,* and many thought that there should be a similar form for women who did not want their marital status to be the first thing people knew about them.

First Lady Jacqueline Kennedy was fairly traditional in the 1960s, but by the 1980s was considered a modern working woman.

National Women's Conference urged the U.S. Congress to support creating jobs for all women who wanted to work and to improve the availability of affordable, quality child care. Despite these efforts, the Equal Rights Amendment failed to be **ratified** in 1982, **falling short** of the needed number of votes by three states.

The 1960s and 1970s were a time of social **liberalism** in the United States, but this changed drastically during the 1980s, when **conservatism** became the nation's foundation. While much of the previous two decades focused on improving the status of many **disadvantaged** groups, the 1980s marked a departure from supporting public programs in favor of national defense and big business—partly fueled by the final stages of the Cold War. President Ronald Reagan was a staunch anti-communist whose pro-capitalist policies **dovetailed** with American fears and sentiments about the Soviet empire. After declaring that it was "morning in America," Reagan made **sweeping** reforms to **eliminated** welfare, pass the largest tax cut in U.S. history, and loosened environmental regulations. Believing that it is not the government's role to provide for individual citizens, he was a **proponent** of supply-side economics. He firmly believed that a smaller government with fewer tax-supported programs meant more wealth for industry, which in turn would create a "trickle-down" effect whereby more jobs and benefits would be created for individuals.

However, this did not prove to be true—especially for the more than nine million immigrants and refugees who arrived in the U.S. between 1980 and 1990, more than at any other time in history. While earlier immigrants had always found work in manufacturing, these high-paid **unionized** jobs were rapidly disappearing due to **outsourcing** and foreign-trade deficits. They were replaced with lower-paying service jobs, causing wages to stagnate. Soon, many families began to realize a need for two incomes to remain firmly middle class. Lack of affordable childcare for working mothers resulted in a generation of **unsupervised** "latchkey" children. Increased family stress contributed to higher divorce rates, leaving a growing number of single parents to make ends meet with less and less money.

As housing, healthcare, and education costs increased, competition for a dwindling number of well-paid jobs fed a **backlash** against Affirmative Action hiring for women and minorities, spurring an **upsurge** in sexism and racism. Conservatives blamed the Feminist Movement for breakdowns in the American family and rallied around the "Moral Majority"—a religiously based, conservative lobbying group. Despite this anti-feminist **climate,** dual career households had become the norm in society, and women were gaining a foothold in public life. The first female justice to the Supreme Court—Sandra Day O'Connor—was appointed in 1981. Sally Ride became the first woman in space in 1983.

While the norms of society were changing, there was also a significant geographic shift in the U.S. population. Families continued to **migrate** to the suburbs and a large number of **retirees** moved to the South and Southwest (an area known as the Sunbelt), leaving cities in rapid decline, crippled by **underperforming** schools, drugs, AIDS, and gang violence. When the Cold War suddenly ended with the fall of the Berlin Wall in 1989, the U.S. was left temporarily as the only world superpower. By the beginning of the 1990s, the economy had begun a rapid recovery with the personal computer industry, dot.com boom, and high-tech advances. High-paying technology jobs allowed suburban yuppies, dual-income couples with no children, and an expanding black middle class to become further removed from the urban working poor and homeless. This economic gap widened even further as middle class households with computers gained Internet access, creating an information divide that further separated the "haves" from the "have nots."

Sandra Day O'Connor, the first woman Supreme Court Justice.

Responding to Information about the U.S. Value Wars

When responding to a reading, it is important to express your opinion and support it based on information from the reading.

Complete these activities.

1. Fill in the first blank of each sentence with an adjective that describes your feeling or opinion.

2. Finish the sentence by adding your own idea. The first one has been done for you as an example.

1. I think discrimination in the workplace is _____ unfair _____

   because _there are many talented working women_.

2. I think an Equal Rights Amendment is _____

   because _____.

3. I think *Roe* v. *Wade* is _____ because

   _____.

4. I think *The Feminist Mystique* is _____ because

   _____.

5. I think the honorifics/forms of address are _____

   because _____.

Understanding the Reading: Comprehension Check

One way to know if you have understood something that you have read is to be able to summarize it in your own words. Write a short letter to an English speaking friend or classmate, narrating and describing what you learned from the reading. Don't worry about using the same order of events or the same words as the reading. Just rewrite the information the way you understand it. You may write your own thoughts and opinions if you want to, but save it for the last paragraph so it doesn't get confused with the information from the reading.

Applying What You Know: An Equality Assessment

Use the survey to assess sensitivity and issues of equality. Give the survey to two class-mates. Use a different color to record each person's answers.

Always   Often   Sometimes   Rarely   Never

1. I refer to men and women by their appropriate social/academic/professional titles.

2. I give proper credit to both men and women who contribute to projects I am involved in.

3. I avoid judging anyone based on social stereotypes, giving each individual the opportunity to be his or her own person.

4. I do not allow others to tell jokes that could be offensive to other genders, races, or cultures in my presence.

5. I take the advice of authority figures (such as doctors or professors) seriously regardless of their gender, race, or ethnic origin.

6. I bring up equality as a discussion topic with my friends, family, and classmates.

7. I respond seriously and thoughtfully to ideas brought up by all individuals— regardless of gender, race, or ethnic origin—in class or in conversations.

8. I support all individuals—regardless of gender, race, or ethnic origin—in achieving their dreams and goals.

Looking at an Autobiography: *Billie Jean* by Billie Jean King

In these paragraphs from her autobiography, tennis star Billie Jean King describes an encounter with an admirer and her feelings about it.

Read this passage.

A strange thing happened back at the Auditorium after I'd finished a light workout. A woman in her early thirties with this odd, intense look in her eyes—she was almost crying—grabbed me by the shoulders and almost before I could say a word told me how she'd been forced to give up athletics when she was a teenager because of pressure from her family. She said she felt foolish even talking to me, but that I was the only idol she'd ever had in her life and she was glad that women finally had somebody of their own sex they could look up to. I didn't know how to answer, I really didn't. I don't even know if she expected an answer. This kind of thing has happened more and more over the last couple of years and I'm always taken aback when it does. It confuses and embarrasses me because I guess I don't really understand what kind of impact I, or my tennis, or my success, or whatever it is, has on other women. But it sure means something to them. Maybe because I've been successful I sometimes forget how tough it is for women to even have the opportunity to succeed. . . . Larry [Larry King, Billie Jean's husband] and I got off on a discussion about the lousy deal girls are still getting in interscholastic sports, something that he and I have talked a lot about lately. It's unbelievable. In 1971 there were 300,000 girls in the entire country in high school sports; in 1973 there were 800,000. Quite a jump until you remember how small the base figure is. . . . Won't there still be lots of frustrated women like the one who talked to me . . . ? (pp. 9–13)

Writing Your Own Brief Autobiography

A *biography* is the story of a person's life written by another person. An *autobiography* contains a person's life story written in first person by the subject. An autobiography has information about your birth, early childhood, and memorable educational or developmental experiences. It also usually contains some reflection on these experiences.

Write a summary of your life, including some reflection on what makes you who you are today. You will be giving this information to a classmate for the next exercise, so only include information that you want to share.

LANGUAGE FOCUS: Using Quoted versus Reported Speech

Representing our own experiences is an important language skill. However, it is also important to know how to represent the experiences of others. In writing, this is accomplished in one of two ways: using direct quotes or using reported speech. In speaking, reported speech is used exclusively. Look at the difference between direct quotes and reported speech.

Direct Quote:	Reported Speech:
Billie Jean King said, "It confuses and embarrasses me because I guess I don't really understand what kind of impact I, or my tennis, or my success, or whatever it is has on other women." • first person pronouns (*I, we*) • *said, "..."* • various tenses	Billie Jean King *said that she was confused* and *embarrassed* because she *didn't* really understand what kind of impact she, or her tennis, or her success, *had* on other women. • third person pronouns (*he, she, they*) • *said that* • past tense forms

Work with a classmate. Exchange autobiographies and write five direct quotes. Then change the quotes into reported speech.

Direct	Indirect
1. Wendy wrote, "I am an ESL teacher."	Wendy wrote that she was an ESL teacher.
2.	
3.	
4.	
5.	

Summarizing

A good summary is usually about 15–20 percent of the length of the original text. Summarizing contains reported speech because it effectively shortens a text and preserves the main ideas. The sample from Billie Jean King's autobiography was about 250 words long. This 50-word summary is 20 percent of the length of the original text.

> Billie Jean wrote that a woman spoke with her and said that she had been forced to give up sports. The woman said that she was glad women had someone to be a role model. Billie Jean wrote that she was embarrassed and that she didn't understand the impact she had on other women.

Summarize your classmate's autobiography by using indirect speech.

LINK TO TODAY: Creating High-Tech Opportunities for All Students

The STEM Education Coalition was founded by Judith A. Ramaley, who formerly served as the director of the National Science Foundation's* education and human-resources division. The coalition is an organization that works with businesses, schools, and legislators to improve education in science, technology, engineering, and math with the goal of maintaining the U.S.'s position as an economic and technological leader in the 21st century global marketplace. The number of students majoring in technology-related fields is decreasing, largely due to poor preparation during elementary and high school. This trend, combined with a large number of retirements in the technology-driven fields that John F. Kennedy and the space race encouraged in the 1960s, is leading to a large potential workforce shortage in engineering and science.

The coalition focuses on congressional lobbying, writing policy, securing funding, training teachers, and recruiting students. There is a high focus on recruiting students from disadvantaged groups, underrepresented minorities, and women, who have traditionally shied away from math and science careers. Expanding the number of highly paid jobs available to women will help close the wage gap between men and women, which is sometimes explained by underrepresentation of women in high-tech fields. One of the key components of the program is mentoring. MentorNet is a non-profit organization that focuses on confidential e-mentoring for women and underrepresented minorities. Another key to the program is to incorporate technology into teaching math and science, creating a "meta" discipline that has components that have historically been taught as separate subjects. The curriculum attempts to level the playing field and teaches males and females equally by encouraging learner-driven classes based on problem solving, discovery, exploration, and scenarios. Teamwork and leadership are core components of the learning.

*National Science Foundation: a government agency that supports research and education in sciences outside of medicine, such as engineering

Fast Facts

- In 1993, women made up 23 percent of the science and engineering workforce. In 2008, they made up 27 percent. Although women have comprised a growing share of the science and engineering workforce, gains have slowed recently. Likewise, other minorities are also under-represented in science and engineering careers. The numbers continue to increase, but at a much slower pace than in the 1990s.[1]

- According to the Population Reference Bureau, women were under-represented in several science and engineering workforces in 2010. They represented only 36 percent in physical science careers, 24 percent of architecture jobs, 25 percent in computer-related fields, and 14 percent in engineering occupations.[2]

- Minorities, such as African Americans and Latinos, in science and engineering occupations, were often working as technicians, jobs that earn less. Chemical technician positions in the science and engineering field had the greatest number of African Americans. The median salary was $43,000 in 2007. Chemists, who were primarily white or Asian, earned $61,000.[3]

Find and read two newspaper, magazine, or Internet articles, one with positive aspects of STEM Education and one detailing the negative aspects. Summarize each article. Then write a short paragraph about your personal conclusions.

positive aspects of STEM education

_____

_____

_____

negative aspects of STEM education

_____

_____

_____

my personal conclusion(s) about STEM Education in the United States

_____

_____

_____

[1] National Science Board. (2012). U.S. S&E workforce: Trends and composition. *Science and Engineering Indicators 2012 Digest.* www.nsf.gov/statistics/digest12/trends.cfm#3.

[2] Population Reference Bureau. (2012). *U.S. science and engineering labor force stalls, but trends vary across states.* http://www.prb.org/Articles/2012/scientists-engineers.aspx.

[3] Population Reference Bureau. (2008). *2007 occupational profiles reveal wide gender, racial gaps in science and engineering employment.* http://www.prb.org/Articles/2008/sloanoccupationpages.aspx.

Putting It All Together

Reflect, and then write your ideas about these questions. Then discuss them in a group.

1. What surprised me most about the information about the feminist movement and the proposed Equal Rights Amendment?

   _____

   _____

2. What does this information help me to understand about modern U.S. American life?

   _____

   _____

3. Does this information change my opinions about U.S. American values and attitudes? How?

   _____

   _____

4. Can people in other countries learn something from the lessons that the United States learned from the conservative–liberal value wars?

   _____

   _____

5. What positive changes can other countries make regarding the role and status of women? Should they make any changes at all?

   _____

   _____

8

The U.S. Enters the 21st Century

Diversity versus Unity in a Rapidly Shifting World

As the U.S. entered a new century, it was faced with trying to balance diversity with unity that continues today. This unit talks about the issues and the country's efforts for balance between two very different concepts.

Net Surfers

To learn more about the time period covered in this unit, search for these names, words, and phrases on the Internet.

electoral college	Osama bin Laden
red states versus blue states	9-11 (9/11)
U.S. war in Afghanistan	World Trade Center Twin Towers
invasion of Iraq	War on Terror

Presidential Suite

George H. W. Bush (R) 1989–1993
William J. (Bill) Clinton (D) 1993–2001
George W. Bush (R) 2001–2009
Barack H. Obama II (D) 2009–

At the Movies

Crash
Hackers
Wag the Dog
Three Kings
In America
Ash Tuesday
Hurt Locker
Remember Me
United 93
World Trade Center

Music Box

"American Idiot"—Green Day
"Let's Roll"—Neil Young
"Only in America"—Brooks and Dunn
"Waiting for the World to Change"—John Mayer
"Where Were You (When the World Stopped Turning)"—Alan Jackson

Preparing to Read about Diversity vs. Unity in a Rapidly Changing World

Write some thoughts about these topics, and then discuss them with your classmates.

1. hate crimes and society

   a. What kinds of hate crimes have been committed in your family's home country?

   _____

   b. What laws, if any, exist regarding hate crimes there?

   _____

   c. Have you had any personal experiences with this issue?

   _____

   _____

2. diversity and public life

   a. What kinds of religious, ethnic, social, or other diversity exist in your family's home country?

   _____

   b. What role does the government have, if any, in protecting or promoting diversity there?

   _____

   c. What is the general public opinion about promoting diversity in that country or community?

   _____

3. national unity

   a. How important is the concept of national unity in your family's home country?

   _____

   _____

   b. What kinds of activities do you think preserve national unity?

   _____

   _____

   c. What kinds of things do you think have a negative effect on it?

   _____

   _____

Learning New Vocabulary about the U.S. as It Enters the 21st Century

Although this is a long list of words to learn, these words will be helpful to understanding the reading. Preview the vocabulary and definitions, and refer to the list as needed.

accommodation (n) modifications that make something more able to be used

brutality (n) the act of being cruel or violent; the use of excessive harmful physical force

disability (n) something that gets in the way of physical or mental function

discourse (n) a large-scale, public-level discussion about or representation of something

dissolution (n) break up or coming apart of something

glitch (n) a bug or problem, especially in a computer program

harassment (n) mistreating someone through annoyance, threats, or demands

hate crime (n) a crime based on a person's affiliation to something

legacy (n) a heritage or something that comes from your history

mobility (n) ability to move to different places

preservation (n) steps taken to keep something functional or alive

supplement (n) extra or additional

telework (n) working from home or off-site—away from the main company

to blur (v) to make fuzzy or to lose focus

to collapse (v) to fall down

to engulf (v) to surround

to usher (v) to introduce something new or accompany somebody/something

relentless (adj) unending

Talking about New Words and Concepts

Take some time to think and talk about new ideas associated with the vocabulary. Then use your understanding of the new vocabulary to discuss each set of questions with a partner.

1. When someone uses excessive physical force against someone else, it is referred to as **brutality.** Many U.S. Americans are concerned about the level of police brutality. Have there ever been instances of police brutality in your community? Describe what you have heard.

   a. Is there an official policy on police brutality in your community? What is it?

   b. Is police brutality justifiable in some cases? When do you think it is OK for police officers to use force? When is it not OK?

   c. List some words that are related to *brutality*.

2. When somebody excessively annoys, threatens, or makes demands of somebody we refer to it as **harassment.** There are many types of harassment, but one of the most discussed forms is sexual harassment in the workplace. This refers to a work environment in which women (or men) are subjected to unwanted attention from members of the opposite sex, such as comments about their bodies, posting of sexually explicit materials, demand of sexual favors as a requisite for keeping their jobs, or sexual advances that need to be returned in exchange for promotions. Efforts to legislate protection against workplace harassment and to prosecute offenders in the U.S. have increased dramatically in recent years.

   a. What kinds of harassment exist in the workplace in your community? What effect do you think that it has on the workers and in the workplace?

   b. Are there any specific laws about or against harassment? If so, what are they and how well are they enforced?

   c. Have you ever experienced harassment personally? If so, in what context? Were you able to do anything to stop the harassment?

   d. List some words that are related to *harassment*.

3. Everything that is circulated in public or in private about an issue is referred to in a broad sense as **discourse,** including written and spoken language, images, and metaphors, among others. Discourse is important because it feeds public opinion about people and issues. Discourse can be manipulated to create public regard for certain issues.

   a. What discourse(s) is/are currently important in your community? Who shapes this/these discourse(s)? Why do they shape it/them in such a manner?

   b. What kinds of negative discourses do you notice in your own community? Positive ones?

   c. What effect can the public have on changing harmful discourses or promoting positive ones?

   d. What effect can you have personally?

   e. List some words that are related to *discourse.*

Before Reading: Relating Concepts

Thinking about the relationship among major concepts before reading can help improve comprehension. Knowing how they work together or against each other activates prior knowledge and helps you make connections.

Use this space here to illustrate the relationships between and among these concepts as you understand them. How do they affect each other? Are they interrelated? Can any of them stand alone?

equality, diversity, inclusion

Reading: The U.S. Enters the 21st Century

The new technologies of the 1980s **ushered** in the Information Age in America, creating a genre of digital media and adding another layer to the poverty gap between those who could afford to have computers and the Internet in their homes and those who could not. The Internet and the information superhighway expanded public access to a rapidly globalizing world. American workers were able to **telework** in larger numbers and the workforce gained more **mobility** as physical job sites became less necessary in some career fields. Online education grew rapidly as a **supplement** and even an alternative to traditional campus learning.

In terms of access and quality of life, advances in technology and software did a great deal to level the playing field for Americans with physical **disabilities**. The 1990 *Americans with Disabilities Act* required workplace human resource departments and university accessibility offices to offer reasonable **accommodations** to workers and students by providing such assistance as interpreters for the hearing impaired, note-takers for the visually impaired, specialized software, and accessible buildings and facilities.

The space shuttle program was something that united Americans in the 1980s and 1990s.

Many credit the rapid increases in the speed and availability of information as one of the factors contributing to the **dissolution** of the Soviet Union, bringing about the end of the Cold War. This left the U.S. as the world's only superpower in the 1990s. Virtually unlimited information access soon popularized a new type of 24-hour, multimedia blitz style of news coverage that was fed by the controversy and buzz of numerous emerging public **discourses.** Some examples included the highly publicized Anita Hill and Clarence Thomas hearings that brought workplace

Citizens show their support for political leaders who share their viewpoints.

harassment into people's living rooms, the Rodney King case and related riots in Los Angeles, and the Louima Case in New York City. These highlighted lingering issues of harassment, racism, or police brutality. The prevalence of **hate crimes** also received wide attention after the beating death of a gay college student, Matthew Shephard, in Wyoming.

Relentless media coverage of these and many other issues began to **blur** the traditional dividing lines between private and public life, affecting everybody from the most anonymous average citizen to inhabitants of the White House. It also served to highlight and vocalize the growing divisions between "red" (conservative/rural-suburban) and "blue" (liberal/urban) values that had begun to quietly **polarize** Americans starting in the 1980s. By the close of the 20th century, U.S. citizens found themselves largely and publically divided in their opinions on domestic issues. This makes the respect of individual personal freedoms guaranteed by the Constitution, the protection of diversity, the **preservation** of tradition, and the issue of national identity and unity among the greatest political and social challenges of the dawning 21st century.

New York City firefighters walk past the U.S. flag after the attack on the World Trade Center on September 11, 2001. (Courtesy of the U.S. Navy.)

The United States began the new millennium with a troublesome **legacy** of its rapid technological growth. The Y2K (Year 2000) scare was a computer programming **glitch** that was predicted to cause chaos and destruction to the country's entire digital network. When the new century arrived without incident, the U.S. returned to its internal debates about the size and role of the government as it related to citizens' private rights versus the need for public responsibility and a common social yardstick against which to measure behavior.

A rapidly decreasing sense of cultural unity or common purpose was decidedly reversed on September 11, 2001, when the United States was tragically reunited against the outside forces that carried out the World Trade Center terrorist attacks in New York City and Washington, DC, and the crash in Pennsylvania. The emerging potential for terrorism had become an issue with the bombings on the World Trade Center in 1993 and the Oklahoma City Federal Building in 1995. However, when the towers collapsed in a massive heap of twisted steel, the U.S. was **engulfed** in a wave of shock, grief, and economic **collapse** that would change public life in 21st century America and impact the future for years to come.

Responding to Information about the U.S. Entering the 21st Century

You have had a glimpse of the U.S. in the first decade of a new millennium. A useful skill to practice is offer opinions about current events.

Based on what you have learned about challenges that the country currently faces as it looks to the next 100 years, complete these sentences with your own ideas and predictions.
   Complete these activities.

1. In the year 2100, the average American will be _____.

2. In the year 2100, daily life in the U.S. will be _____

_____.

3. In the year 2100, the mood in the U.S. will be _____.

4. In the year 2100, the site of the World Trade Center in New York City will be occupied

   by _____.

5. In the year 2100, technology will allow Americans to _____

_____.

6. In the year 2100, the role of the U.S. in the world will be _____

_____.

Understanding the Reading: Comprehension Check

Retelling information from reading is probably one of the most difficult skills to learn in a foreign language.

Without looking back, take a few moments to write some notes about the reading in your own words. Then, with your books closed, retell the information to a classmate as you understand it.

_____

_____

_____

_____

_____

_____

Applying What You Know: Taking a Diversity Sensitivity Assessment

Use the survey to assess diversity sensitivity. Give the survey to two classmates. Use a different color to record each person's answers.

| Always | Usually | Sometimes | Rarely | Never |

1. I speak out against stereotypes and stereotyping in public settings.

2. If I notice discrimination happening around me, I say something about it.

3. I choose topics related to diversity for community projects, academic research, class projects, and informal conversation.

4. I keep an open mind toward others' thoughts, beliefs, attitudes, and emotions.

5. I make myself familiar with the cultural practices of various community groups.

6. I am aware of my own prejudices and consciously avoid acting on them.

Memorializing a Nation: Looking at Monuments in Washington, DC

Arlington National Cemetery near Washington, DC.

The manner in which a country chooses to immortalize its heroes and landmark events is an important indicator of public values and beliefs. Washington, DC, has many memorials and monuments to former presidents such as George Washington, Abraham Lincoln, Thomas Jefferson, and Franklin D. Roosevelt. Events such as World War I, World War II, Vietnam, Korea, and others are also memorialized. Significant sites also exist outside of the capital, such as Ground Zero in New York City or the federal building in Oklahoma City.

Read about these monuments and memorials currently open to the public in the nation's capital city.

- African-American Civil War Memorial and Museum: Wall of Honor listing names of 209,145 United States Colored Troops from the Civil War

- Arlington National Cemetery: America's largest burial ground includes the grave of President John F. Kennedy

- DC War Memorial: Commemorates the 26,000 citizens of Washington, DC, who served in World War I

- Eisenhower Memorial: Grove of oak trees, huge limestone columns, and a semicircular space made, monolithic stone blocks and carvings and inscriptions that depict images of Eisenhower's life

- Franklin Delano Roosevelt Memorial: Four outdoor sculpture galleries— one for each of FDR's terms in office from 1933 to 1945

- George Mason Memorial: Monument to the Virginia man who influenced the Bill of Rights

- Iwo Jima Memorial: United States Marine Corps War Memorial dedicated to the battle of Iwo Jima

- Jefferson Memorial: The 19-foot bronze statue of Jefferson located on the Tidal Basin, surrounded by a grove of trees
- Korean War Veterans Memorial: Nineteen figures represent every ethnic background with 2,400 faces of land, sea, and air support troops
- Lady Bird Johnson Memorial Grove: The grove of trees and 15 acres of gardens honors the former first lady's role in beautifying the country's landscape
- Lincoln Memorial: Honors the nation's Civil War president and gives words to the Gettysburg Address
- Martin Luther King Jr. National Memorial: Granite structure that honors Dr. King's vision of freedom, opportunity, and justice
- National Law Enforcement Officers Memorial: Honors the service and sacrifice of more than 17,000 federal, state, and local law enforcers
- Pentagon Memorial: Honors the 184 lives lost in the Pentagon and on American Airlines Flight 77 during the terrorist attacks on September 11, 2001
- Theodore Roosevelt Island: 91-acre wilderness preserve serves as a memorial to the nation's 26th president, honoring his contributions to conservation of public lands for forests, national parks, and wildlife preserves
- United States Air Force Memorial: Honors millions of men and women who have served in U.S. air forces
- U.S. Holocaust Memorial Museum: Serves as a memorial to the millions of people who were murdered during the Holocaust
- United States Navy Memorial: Commemorates U.S. Naval history and honors all who have served in the sea services
- Vietnam Veterans Memorial: Granite wall inscribed with names of 58,209 Americans missing or killed during the Vietnam War (see photo on page 118)
- Washington Monument: Dedicated in 1885 to honor the first president of the United States—George Washington
- Women in Vietnam Memorial: Sculpture depicting three military nurses with a wounded soldier to honor the women who served in the Vietnam War
- World War II Memorial: Outdoor pool and bronze star collection commemorates those who served in World War II

LANGUAGE FOCUS: Using Compare and Contrast Transition Words

The memorials in Washington, DC, are similar in some ways and different in others. Think of two memorials you are familiar with. Write five descriptive sentences about each one.

Memorial 1	Memorial 2

Learning compare and contrast transition words is helpful because they are commonly used by U.S. American English speakers to connect ideas and information about things that are similar and different. Learning to use these words effectively can help you to speak and write more academically. Transition words used for comparing usually point out similarities, whereas transitions used for contrasting point out differences. Common transition words and phrases include:

Compare	Contrast
by the same token	*but*
equally	*conversely*
in a like manner	*however*
in the same way	*on the other hand*
likewise	*whereas*
similarly	*while*
	yet

Both compare and contrast transition words are used to connect the ideas of two complete, independent clauses to form a stronger relationship between the sentences. The transition word can be used at the beginning of the second sentence.

> Example (Comparing): *The Washington Memorial is made of white marble. In a like manner, the Lincoln memorial is also made of white marble.*

> Example (Contrasting): *The Washington Memorial is an abstract shape. On the other hand, the Lincoln Memorial depicts a real person.*

Use the descriptive sentences you wrote and expand them into sentences that compare and contrast the properties, contents, or feelings evoked by the memorials you chose.

1.

2.

3.

4.

5.

6.

7.

8.

9.

10.

Expressing and Supporting Your Own Opinions about Public Representation via Memorials

U.S. American English speakers often begin their own opinions with phrases that let listeners know they are about to hear an opinion.

Think about the memorials again. The beginnings of some sentences that express opinions are listed. Finish each with your own interpretation(s) of what it conveys to the public.

1. I believe this memorial conveys the message that . . .

2. I think that the artist created this memorial because . . .

3. My opinion about the artist's depiction is that it. . . .

4. I like/dislike the memorial because. . . .

LANGUAGE FOCUS: Agreeing and Disagreeing

When people have different opinions, it is often necessary to note whether you agree with some aspect of what the other person is saying, or whether you completely disagree before giving your own opinion. Certain phrases are commonly used.

Partial Agreement	Complete Disagreement
Yes, but I think that	I disagree because
Yes, but I believe that	I see it differently because
Yes, but I feel that	I don't think so because

Some of the national monuments have been controversial in terms of what they show, for example, as a president's legacy. The issues about Franklin Roosevelt's memorial centered on how the former president—who had polio as an adult and who used a wheelchair—should be shown.

Here is an example of an exchange that shows partial agreement with the speaker's opinion about the FDR memorial.

FDR Memorial

Speaker 1: *I dislike this statue because the wheels on the wheelchair are too big.*

Speaker 2: *Yes, but I feel that the wheelchair is still important.*

Here is an example of an exchange that shows complete disagreement with the speaker's opinion about the memorial.

Speaker 1: *I believe that this statue conveys the message that wheelchairs are not publicly accepted.*

Speaker 2: *I disagree because Roosevelt himself did not want to be portrayed in his wheelchair. The statue is respectful of his personal wishes.*

Work with a partner in class using your opinion sentences. If possible, bring a picture of it to class. Look at each other's opinions.

1. Which ones do you partially agree with? Which ones do you completely disagree with?

2. Practice responding to each of your partner's sentences using one of the phrases listed in the box on page 164.

LINK TO TODAY: Ground Zero and the Freedom Tower

Lower Manhattan's World Trade Center site consists of 16 acres of land owned primarily by the Port Authority of New York. The complex and its seven office towers was destroyed on September 11, 2001, when terrorists flew two hijacked planes into the two largest towers, Tower 1 (North) and Tower 2 (South), both of which collapsed within two hours. Falling debris from the North Tower caught the smaller Tower 7 on fire, and the thousands of tons of dust, debris, and wreckage ultimately made the entire site uninhabitable. The New York City Mayor at the time, Rudy Giuliani, stated, "We will rebuild. We're going to come out of this stronger than before, politically stronger, economically stronger. The skyline will be made whole again."

In November 2001, the Lower Manhattan Development Corporation was formed to oversee the rebuilding and to coordinate between the Port Authority, the architects, and the victims' families. In December 2001, a public viewing platform was installed. In March 2002, the Tribute of Light was added, forming two beams of light shooting straight into the sky. They are lit every year on the anniversary of the attack. Cleaning was completed by May 2002 and in August of the same year, an international design competition for the site was announced. Amid controversy, New York governor at the time, George Pataki, chose Studio Daniel Libeskind's Memory Foundations as the site's master plan in 2003. Central to the design is a memorial called "Reflecting Absence" by Peter Walker and architect Michael Arad. Two square pools designating the site of the original twin towers sit amid a field of trees and walls bearing the names of the victims. The memorial was dedicated on September 11, 2011. One World Trade Center ("Freedom Tower") was started in April 2006. When completed, its radio antenna will make it the world's tallest all-office building in the western hemisphere.[1]

David Childs of Skidmore, Owings and Merrill designed Tower Seven, which opened in May 2006. Groundbreaking for Richard Rogers Partnership's Tower Three, which stands across from the reflecting pools, is scheduled for completion in 2014. Ground was broken for British architect Norman Foster's Tower Two with its diamond shaped roof in July 2008. Construction on Maki and Associates' Tower Four began in 2008. In 2011, Kohn Pederson Fox's Tower Five was started. In 2010, victims' families were outraged by plans to build a mosque and an Islamic center two blocks from the site of the 9/11 attacks that were carried out by men affiliated with Al-Qaeda, an Islamic terrorist organization. Despite angry protest, a Lower Manhattan community board voted to move ahead with the plans to help make the U.S. a more racially and ethnically diverse land. The entire Ground Zero site is expected to be fully rebuilt and occupied sometime around the year 2037.

---

[1] Skyscraperpage.com. (2012). *World skyscraper construction 2012.* Skyscraperpage.com/diagrams/?searchID=202.

Fast Facts

- According to an article by Jennifer M. Ortman and Christine E. Guarneri, the United States population will experience a large increase in racial and ethnic diversity, due in part to migration.[2]

- More than half the growth in the U.S. population between 2000 and 2010 can be attributed to the growth in the Hispanic population. In 2010, there were 50.5 million Hispanics in the United States, which accounts for 16 percent of the total population.[3]

- In 1970, the Hispanic population was 9.6 million. It has steadily increased every decade and is projected to be 59.7 million in 2020 and 102.6 million by the year 2050.[4]

- The foreign-born population in the United States is changing. Before 2005, most of the foreign-born population came from the Caribbean, Central America, or South America to total 54.2 percent. Since 2008, the percentage of people who entered from Asia increased from 26.9 percent prior to 2005 to 40.3 percent after 2008. The Hispanic population decreased to 40.7 percent after 2008. The African population has increased from 3.5 percent prior to 2005 to 6.2 percent between 2005 and 2007 and to 6.6 percent in 2008 and beyond. The European population is the only one that has decreased. It began at 12.8 percent prior to 2005, but then dropped to 8.0 percent between 2005 and 2007 before increasing to 9.1 percent in 2008 and beyond.[5]

---

[2] Ortman, Jennifer M. and Guarneri, Christine E. (2009). *United States population projections: 2000 to 2050.* www.census.gov/population/www/projections/analytical-document09.pdf.

[3] U.S. Census Bureau. (2011). *The 2010 Census brief: Overview of race and hispanic origin.* www.census.gov/prod/cen2010/briefs/c2010br-02.pdf.

[4] U.S. Census Bureau. (2011). *Hispanic population of the United States.* www.census.gov/population/www/socdemo/hispanic/hispanic_pop_presentation.html.

[5] U.S. Census Bureau. (2011). *The newly arrived foreign-born population of the United States: 2010.* http://www.census.gov/prod/2011pubs/acsbr10-16.pdf.

Find and read two newspaper, magazine, or Internet articles, one with positive aspects of racial and ethnic diversity and one detailing the negative aspects. Summarize each article. Then write a short pargraph about your personal conclusions.

positive aspects of racial and ethnic diversity

_____

_____

_____

_____

negative aspects of racial and ethnic diversity

_____

_____

_____

_____

my personal conclusion(s) about racial and ethnic diversity in the United States

_____

_____

_____

_____

Putting It All Together

Reflect, and then write your ideas about these questions. Then discuss them in a group.

1. What surprised me most about the information on diversity and inclusion in the United States?

   _____

   _____

2. What does this information help me to understand about modern U.S. American life?

   _____

   _____

3. Does this information change my opinions about U.S. American values and attitudes? How?

   _____

   _____

4. Can people in other countries learn something from the experiences U.S. Americans had with diversity? If so, what?

   _____

   _____

5. What will I tell people if they ask me about persons with disabilities in the United States?

   _____

   _____

6. What positive changes can other countries make regarding accessibility for all people? Should they make any changes at all?

   _____

   _____